Math Workout for the

SAT®

4th Edition

By Jonathan Chiu and the Staff of The Princeton Review

PrincetonReview.com

Penguin
Random
House

The Princeton Review
555 W. 18th Street
New York, NY 10011
E-mail: editorialsupport@review.com

Published in the United States by Penguin Random House
LLC, New York, and in Canada by Random House of Canada,
a division of Penguin Random House Ltd., Toronto.

Terms of Service: The Princeton Review Online Companion
Tools ("Student Tools") for retail books are available for only
the two most recent editions of that book. Student Tools may
be activated only twice per eligible book purchased for two
consecutive 12-month periods, for a total of 24 months of
access. Activation of Student Tools more than twice per book
is in direct violation of these Terms of Service and may result
in discontinuation of access to Student Tools Services.

ISBN: 978-1-101-92053-4
eBook ISBN: 978-1-101-92068-8
ISSN: 1551-6431

SAT is a registered trademark of the College Board, which is
not affiliated with The Princeton Review.

The Princeton Review is not affiliated with Princeton
University.

Editor: Aaron Riccio
Production Editor: Liz Rutzel
Production Artist: Gabriel Berlin

Printed in the United States of America on partially recycled
paper.

10 9 8 7 6 5 4 3 2 1

Fourth Edition

Editorial

Rob Franek, Senior VP, Publisher
Casey Cornelius, VP Content Development
Mary Beth Garrick, Director of Production
Selena Coppock, Managing Editor
Meave Shelton, Senior Editor
Colleen Day, Editor
Sarah Litt, Editor
Aaron Riccio, Editor
Orion McBean, Editorial Assistant

Penguin Random House Publishing Team

Tom Russell, VP, Publisher
Alison Stoltzfus, Publishing Director
Jake Eldred, Associate Managing Editor
Ellen Reed, Production Manager
Suzanne Lee, Designer

Acknowledgments

This book could not have been built without the hard work and dedication of Christina Bonvicino, Chris Chimera, Amy Minster, and Jonathan Chiu.

Additionally, The Princeton Review would like to thank Gabriel Berlin for diligently deciphering our notes and translating them into the clean copy seen within this book, and Liz Rutzel for scouring the interiors for errors.

Special thanks to Adam Robinson, who conceived of and perfected the Joe Bloggs approach to standardized tests and many of the other successful techniques used by the Princeton Review.

Contents

Register Your

1 Go to **PrincetonReview.com/cracking**

2 You'll see a welcome page where you can register your book using the following ISBN: 9781101920534

3 After placing this free order, you'll either be asked to log in or to answer a few simple questions in order to set up a new Princeton Review account.

4 Finally, click on the "Student Tools" tab located at the top of the screen. It may take an hour or two for your registration to go through, but after that, you're good to go.

If you are experiencing book problems (potential content errors), please contact EditorialSupport@review.com with the full title of the book, its ISBN number (located above), and the page number of the error. Experiencing technical issues? Please e-mail TPRStudentTech@review.com with the following information:

- your full name
- e-mail address used to register the book
- full book title and ISBN
- your computer OS (Mac or PC) and Internet browser (Firefox, Safari, Chrome, etc.)
- description of technical issue

Book Online!

Once you've registered, you can...

- Find any late-breaking information about the SAT.

- Get valuable advice about the college-application process, including tips for writing a great essay and where to apply for financial aid.

- Sort colleges by whatever you're looking for (such as Best Theater, Best Dorm, or Top Notch Professors), learn more about your top choices, and see how they rank according to *The Best 381 Colleges.*

- Check to see if there have been any corrections or updates to this edition.

Look For These Icons Throughout The Book

Proven Techniques

Applied Strategies

Student-Produced Response

Calculator Permitted

The **Princeton** Review®

Introduction

IN THE BEGINNING . . .

Even though the SAT is designed for juniors and seniors, most of the math on the test bears little resemblance to the type of math found in the high school classroom. Many students find it hard to believe—not to mention a little humiliating—that a test that seems so difficult actually tests little more than basic algebra, arithmetic, and geometry. Even students who are very good at math in school often have trouble on the SAT. Why?

The fact is that while the SAT uses basic mathematical concepts, it's unlike any math test you will ever see in school. The SAT uses basic math problems in very particular ways. This is why preparing for the SAT requires a new set of skills. The SAT does not test how smart you are, how well you will do in school, or what kind of person you are. It only tests *how well you do on the SAT*. And doing well on the SAT is a skill that can be learned.

How can you improve your score on the SAT? First, you need to learn the structure of the test. This will help you develop an overall test-taking strategy. Then you need to learn some powerful test-taking skills, which will help you think your way through SAT-type problems.

Some of our advice may sound a little strange. In fact, if you try some of our techniques in math class, your teacher will probably be unhappy. But remember, this isn't math class. This is the SAT, and it's your job to get as good at SAT math as you can.

Structure of the Math Sections

Of the four scored multiple-choice sections on the SAT, two of them will be math. The questions will be presented in two different formats: regular multiple choice and grid-ins. We will discuss how to deal with each of these question formats.

How to Use this Book

This book is designed for students who want concentrated math preparation. It can be used alone or as a supplement to our *Cracking the SAT*. While we will briefly review the essential Princeton Review test-taking strategies and problem-solving skills, if you want an in-depth guide to these techniques, you'll want to also read *Cracking the SAT*.

Where Does the SAT Come From?

The SAT is published by the Educational Testing Service (ETS) under the sponsorship of the College Entrance Examination Board (the College Board). ETS and the College Board are both private companies.

WHAT IS THE PRINCETON REVIEW?

The Princeton Review is one of the nation's premier test-preparation companies. We have conducted courses in hundreds of locations around the country, and we prepare more students for the SAT than anyone else. We also prepare students for the PSAT/NMSQT, ACT, GRE, GMAT, LSAT, MCAT, and other standardized tests.

The Princeton Review's techniques are unique and powerful. We developed them after spending countless hours scrutinizing real SATs, analyzing them with computers, and proving our theories with real students.

This book is based on our extensive experience in the classroom. Our techniques for cracking the SAT will help you improve your SAT scores by teaching you to:

1. think like the test writers at ETS and the College Board

2. take full advantage of the limited time allowed

3. find the answers to questions you don't understand by guessing intelligently

4. avoid the traps that ETS and the College Board have laid for you (and use those traps to your advantage)

Chapter 1
Strategies

We'll say it again: This isn't the kind of test you get in math class. You need some special techniques for handling SAT problems—techniques that will help you go faster and that take advantage of the format of the questions. Some of the things we suggest may seem awkward at first, so practice them. If you do the math questions on the SAT the way your math teacher taught you, you waste time and throw away points.

ORDER OF DIFFICULTY

In order to formulate a test-taking strategy, it can be helpful to understand the breakdown of the two math sections. The questions are arranged in a rough order of difficulty, with most easier questions at the beginning of each section and most harder questions at the end. The majority of the test tends to be at a medium difficulty, somewhere between these two extremes. To better help you practice, we've included a variety of problems that give you exposure to questions of all types and categories, approximating the College Board's easy, medium, and hard categories. Your individual approach will likely differ in some areas, which is why we also suggest using the following section to craft an ideal approach.

POOD (Personal Order of Difficulty)

Some questions will be easier for you than others, based on your personal strengths and weaknesses. Use this to your advantage! For example, if you struggle with fractions, skip over those questions in favor of ones you know you can get right. It's all about your POOD!

PACING

Almost everybody works too fast on the SAT, losing a lot of points due to careless errors. The SAT isn't your usual math situation—you don't get *partial credit* for "having the right idea." The only thing that matters is what you bubble in on your answer sheet. Slow down! If you find yourself making careless mistakes, you are throwing points out the window.

Unless you're shooting for a score of 700 or above, do not finish the math sections. Again, this isn't like math class. The test isn't designed for you to finish, and you'll hurt your score by trying to do so. If you miss a total of around five or six questions in both sections, you're probably hitting the right pace. More mistakes than that, and you're going too quickly. If you aren't missing any questions but aren't finishing, you should guess more aggressively and try to work a bit faster. Use the following breakdown of questions to get a sense for how much time you might want to spend on each. See how that time changes if you choose to skip certain questions entirely.

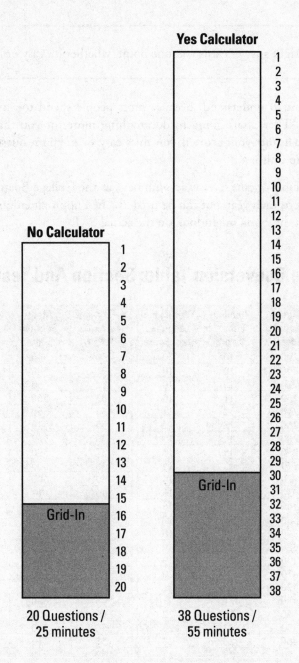

Yes Calculator

1
2
3
4
5
6
7
8
9
10
11
12
13
14
15
16
17
18
19
20
21
22
23
24
25
26
27
28
29
30
31
32
33
34
35
36
37
38

Grid-In

No Calculator

1
2
3
4
5
6
7
8
9
10
11
12
13
14
15
16
17
18
19
20

Grid-In

20 Questions /
25 minutes

38 Questions /
55 minutes

SCORING AND LOTD (LETTER OF THE DAY)

If you were betting your hard-earned cash, wouldn't you want to know the odds? On the SAT, you're betting for more points, and it's important to understand how the scoring works so you'll play smart.

For each right answer, you earn one raw point. If you answer a question incorrectly, nothing happens. There is no penalty for guessing! Take advantage of this. You still want to eliminate questions that you know are wrong, to increase your chances of guessing the right one, but if you run out of time, just choose a Letter of the Day (LOTD) and fill in it for all remaining questions. This will increase the odds of getting some questions right. Never leave a question blank!

> Every right answer earns you one point, whether it's easy or hard.

That's important to understand, because most people spend too much time on hard questions. They aren't going to do anything more for you than easy questions—and you'll hurt your score if you miss easy or medium questions because you're rushing to finish.

The following table doesn't have exact numbers, as the College Board makes individual adaptations each year, but can be used as a best approximation of how your raw scores from this book might look on the actual SAT.

Raw Score Conversion Table: Section And Test Scores

Raw Score (# of correct answers)	Math Section Score	Reading Test Score	Writing and Language Test Score	Raw Score (# of correct answers)	Math Section Score	Reading Test Score	Writing and Language Test Score
0	200	10	10	30	530	28	29
1	200	10	10	31	540	28	30
2	210	10	10	32	550	29	30
3	230	11	10	33	560	29	31
4	240	12	11	34	560	30	32
5	260	13	12	35	570	30	32
6	280	14	13	36	580	31	33
7	290	15	13	37	590	31	34
8	310	15	14	38	600	32	34
9	320	16	15	39	600	32	35
10	330	17	16	40	610	33	36
11	340	17	16	41	620	33	37
12	360	18	17	42	630	34	38
13	370	19	18	43	640	35	39
14	380	19	19	44	650	35	40
15	390	20	19	45	660	36	
16	410	20	20	46	670	37	
17	420	21	21	47	670	37	
18	430	21	21	48	680	38	
19	440	22	22	49	690	38	
20	450	22	23	50	700	39	
21	460	23	23	51	710	40	
22	470	23	24	52	730	40	
23	480	24	25	53	740		
24	480	24	25	54	750		
25	490	25	26	55	760		
26	500	25	26	56	780		
27	510	26	27	57	790		
28	520	26	28	58	800		
29	520	27	28				

Conversion Equation: Section And Test Scores

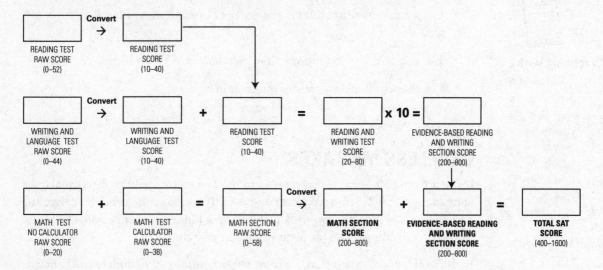

Amazing, isn't it? Even to get a very high score, *you don't have to finish.* Accuracy is more important than speed! Slow down and score more!

POE (PROCESS OF ELIMINATION)

Throughout this book, always look for opportunities to eliminate wrong answers. Each time you do so, you make it easier to pick out the right answer, especially if you have to guess. If you see something wrong, eliminate it.

CALCULATORS

Seems like a good deal, doesn't it? Well, maybe. It depends on the test section. Even for the portion of the test for which calculators are allowed, make sure you know how you're going to solve the problem before you just start running random calculations.

> Calculators can only calculate; they can't think. You need to figure out how to solve the problem before you can begin calculating.

Calculators are great for helping you avoid silly mistakes in your arithmetic, and you should use them when you can. They can help ensure that you make correct calculations, but they can't tell you which calculations are the right ones to make.

Calcu-later

The first of the two math sections does not permit the use of calculators. ETS and the College Board are specifically measuring how students will perform without electronic help. Don't panic! Many of the techniques in this book will make these questions more straightforward. To make sure you're practicing a mix of skills, only use the calculator when you see the calculator symbol.

Practicing With a Calculator

Not every problem on the calculator section is best solved with the calculator. That said, you should try solving the questions indicated in this book with the calculator icon shown above so that you have a better sense of when it's more efficient for you not to use it.

Tips to Calculator Happiness

- Get a calculator that follows the order of operations and has keys for x^2, y^x, and $\sqrt{\ }$.

- Use the same calculator every time you practice SAT problems.

- Check each number after you punch it in.

CARELESS MISTAKES

If you are prone to careless mistakes—and most of us are—you probably make the same kinds of careless mistakes over and over. If you take the time to analyze the questions you get wrong, you will discover which kinds are your personal favorites. Then you can compensate for them when you take the SAT.

In the world, and in math class, it's most important for you to understand concepts and ways to solve problems. On the SAT, it's most important that you bubble in the correct answer. Students typically lose anywhere from 30 to 100 points simply by making careless, preventable mistakes.

Some common mistakes to watch for:

- misreading the question

- computation error

- punching in the wrong thing on the calculator

- on a medium or hard question, stopping after one or two steps, when the question requires three or four steps

- answering a different question from the one asked

If, for example, you find you keep missing questions because you multiply wrong, then do every multiplication twice. Do every step on paper, not in your head. If you make a lot of mistakes on positive/negative, write out each step, and be extra careful on those questions. Correcting careless mistakes is an easy way to pick up more points, so make sure you analyze your mistakes so you know what to look out for.

PLUGGING IN

One of the most powerful math techniques on the SAT is called Plugging In. The idea of Plugging In is to take all of the variables—things like x, y, z—in a problem and replace them with actual numbers. This turns your algebra problems into simple arithmetic and can make even the hardest problem an easy one.

How To Recognize a Plugging-In Question

- There are variables in the answer choices.

- The question says something like *in terms of x*.

- Your first thought is to write an equation.

- The question asks for a percentage or fractional part of something, but it doesn't give you any actual amounts.

How To Solve a Plugging-In Question

- Don't write an equation.

- Pick an easy number and substitute it for the variable.

- Work the problem through and get an answer. Circle it so you don't lose track of it.

- Plug in your number—the one you chose in the beginning—to the answer choices and see which choice produces your circled answer.

Here's an example:

> **4**
>
> Jill spent x dollars on pet toys and 12 dollars on socks. If the amount Jill spent was twice the amount she earns each week, how much does Jill earn each week in terms of x ?
>
> A) $2(x + 12)$
>
> B) $2x + 24$
>
> C) $\dfrac{x}{2} + 12$
>
> D) $\dfrac{x + 12}{2}$

Solution: Plug in 100 for x. That means Jill spent a total of 112 dollars. If that was twice her weekly salary, then she makes half of 112, or 56 dollars a week. Circle 56. Now plug 100 into the answers to see which one yields 56. Choice (A) is 2(100 + 12) = 224. No good. Choice (B) is 224, which is also too big. Choice (C) is 50 + 12 = 62. Choice (D) = 56! Yes! The answer is (D). Here's a more complicated example:

11

Kimberly and Elizabeth are having lunch at a diner. The price of Kimberly's meal is z dollars, and the price of Elizabeth's meal is $4 more than the price of Kimberly's meal. They decide to evenly share the cost of lunch, and a 10% tax is applied to the meal. Which of the following expressions represents the amount, in dollars, that each of them owes, without tip?

A) $0.1z + 4.0$

B) $1.1z + 2.2$

C) $2.2z + 4.4$

D) $4.2z + 0.1$

Solution: Start by picking a value for the variable z. Let's say Kimberly's meal was $10, so $z = 10$. Elizabeth's meal was $4 more, or $14, for a total of $24. The 10% tax would add another $2.40 for a grand total of $26.40. When they split that, each will owe $13.20. Circle that number: It is the target number that answers this question. Now go to the answer choices and plug in 10 for z. Whichever one matches the target is the correct answer. Choice (A) becomes $0.1(10) + 4 = 1 + 4 = 5$, so eliminate it. Choice (B) becomes $1.1(10) + 2.2 = 11 + 2.2 = 13.2$, which matches the target number. Don't stop there, though! Occasionally, more than one answer will match the target number, so always check all four just to be sure. If more than one matches, you can just pick new values for the variables and check the remaining answers. Choice (C) becomes $2.2(10) + 4.4 = 22 + 4.4 = 26.4$, and (D) becomes $4.2(10) + 0.1 = 42 + 0.1 = 42.1$. Neither of these matches the target, so (B) is the correct answer. Notice how the value of (C) was the grand total for the meal. You might have chosen this if you missed that Kimberly and Elizabeth were splitting the cost of the meal. Make sure to read carefully to avoid careless mistakes and trap answers.

Here's a different kind of example:

8

At his bake sale, Mr. Heftwhistle sold 30% of his pies to one friend. Mr. Heftwhistle then sold 60% of the remaining pies to another friend. What percent of his original number of pies did Mr. Heftwhistle have left?

A) 10%

B) 18%

C) 28%

D) 36%

Solution: If you don't plug in, you may make the sad mistake of picking (A) or of working with ugly fractions. Plugging in a number is much easier. Let's say Mr. Heftwhistle had 100 pies. 30% of 100 equals 30, so he's left with 70. 60% of 70 equals 42, so he's left with 28. Here's the great thing about plugging in 100 on percentage problems—28 (left) out of 100 (original number) is simply 28%. That's it. Choice (C) is the answer.

Tips for Plugging In Happiness

- Pick easy numbers like 2, 4, 10, 100. The best number to choose depends on the question. For example, use 100 for percents.

- Avoid picking 0, 1, or any number that shows up in the answer choices.

- If the number you picked leads to ugly computations—fractions, negatives, or anything you need a calculator for—bail out and pick an easier number.

- Practice!

On the next page is a Quick Quiz, so you can practice Plugging In before you continue. Answers and explanations immediately follow every Quick Quiz.

QUICK QUIZ #1

Easy

5

If $\dfrac{c-d}{c} = \dfrac{5}{8}$, which of the following must also be true?

A) $\dfrac{c-d}{d} = \dfrac{8}{5}$

B) $\dfrac{d}{c} = \dfrac{13}{8}$

C) $\dfrac{c+d}{c} = \dfrac{13}{8}$

D) $\dfrac{c}{d} = \dfrac{8}{3}$

Medium

13

If $\dfrac{y}{3} = 6x$, then in terms of y, which of the following is equivalent to x ?

A) $2y$

B) y

C) $\dfrac{y}{2}$

D) $\dfrac{y}{18}$

Hard

29

$$2x + p = 7x - 3$$

$$2y + q = 7y - 3$$

In the above equations, p and q are constants. If q is 5 less than p, which of the following statements is true?

A) x is 1 less than y

B) x and y are equal

C) x is 1 more than y

D) x is 2 more than y

Answers and Explanations: Quick Quiz #1

5. **C** Plugging in is all about making your life easier, so do the easiest thing here and make $c = 8$. Now figure out what value of d makes the equation true. The numerators must be equal, so $8 - d = 5$ and $d = 3$. Use these values to test the answer choices. Choice (A) becomes $\frac{8-5}{5} = \frac{8}{5}$, which is not true. Choice (B) becomes $\frac{5}{8} = \frac{13}{8}$, which can be eliminated. Choice (C) becomes $\frac{8+5}{8} = \frac{13}{8}$, which is true, and (D) becomes $\frac{8}{5} = \frac{8}{3}$, which is false. Only (C) is true, so that's the correct answer.

13. **D** Plug in $y = 36$, which makes $x = 2$. Now plug in 36 for y in the answer choices and look for x, which is 2. Choice (A) is something huge. Choice (B) is 36. Choice (C) is 18, which is still too big. Choice (D) is 2, so (D) is correct.

29. **C** There is a lot more going on in this question, so write things down to avoid confusion. Start with q and p since their relationship is given. If $p = 7$, then $q = 2$. Plug these values into the equations and solve for x and y. The first equation becomes $2x + 7 = 7x - 3$ or $5x = 10$, so $x = 2$. The second equation becomes $2y + 2 = 7y - 3$ or $5y = 5$, so $y = 1$. Use POE to get rid of answers that aren't true. All but (C) are false, so (C) is the correct answer.

In Question 13, you may have had a hard time coming up with numbers that worked evenly. That's OK—it takes practice. You can plug in any numbers you want, as long as they satisfy the conditions of the problem, so you might as well plug in numbers that are easy to work with.

In Question 29, you could have solved this without plugging in, but then you'd be dealing with a whole lot of algebraic manipulation. It would be easy to get lost or make a mistake while solving and substituting. Plugging in real numbers lets you turn ugly algebra into simple arithmetic problems. Use it any time you are having trouble imagining how the numbers behave. Another example of a situation in which you will be better off with concrete numbers is when you are asked for some percent or fractional part of an unknown total. Making that total a real number will make it easier to deal with.

PLUGGING IN THE ANSWER CHOICES

Good news. Unlike the math tests you usually have in school, the SAT is primarily multiple choice. That means that on many problems, you don't have to generate your own answer to a problem. Instead, the answer will be one of the four answers sitting on the page right in front of you. All you have to figure out is which one is the answer.

How to Recognize Questions for Plugging In the Answer Choices

- The question will be straightforward—something like "How old is Bob?" or "How many potatoes are in the bag?" or "What was the original cost of the stereo?"

- The answer choices will be actual values.

How to Plug In the Answer Choices

Don't write an equation. Instead, pick an answer and work it through the steps of the problem, one at a time, and see if it works. In essence, you're asking *what if (C) is the answer? Does that solve the problem?*

Here's an example:

7

If $\dfrac{3(x-1)}{2} = \dfrac{9}{x-2}$, what is the value of x ?

A) −4

B) −2

C) 1

D) 4

Solution: Start with one of the answers in the middle. Let's try (C) first. Plug in 1 for x and see if the equation works:

$$\frac{3(1-1)}{2} = \frac{9}{1-2}$$

$$\frac{0}{2} = \frac{9}{-1}$$

Okay, so (C) isn't the answer. Cross it out. Try (D):

$$\frac{3(4-1)}{2} = \frac{9}{4-2}$$

$$\frac{9}{2} = \frac{9}{2}$$

The equation works, so (D) is the answer. Sure, you could have done the algebra, but wasn't plugging in easier? Once again, you've seen an algebra problem turned into an arithmetic problem, and all it required was managing simple operations like $4 - 1$. You're much more likely to make mistakes dealing with x than with $4 - 1$. Also, when you plug in, you're taking advantage of the fact that there are only four answer choices. One of them is correct. You might as well try them and find out which one it is—and you no longer have to face the horror of working out a problem algebraically and finding that your answer isn't one of the choices.

Here's a harder example:

> **20**
>
> A store sells shirts for $7.50 each and hats for $5.00 each. The store earns $1,822.50 in one day from selling a total of 307 shirts and hats. How many shirts were sold on that day?
>
> A) 37
> B) 89
> C) 115
> D) 202

Solution: Start by labeling your answers and the other parts of the problem to keep your work organized in a chart, like this:

shirts	earnings from shirts	hats	earnings from hats	total earnings

A) 37

B) 89

C) 115

D) 202

Try (B) first and fill the numbers into the chart as you go. If the store sold 89 shirts, it would earn 89 × $7.50 = $667.50 from them. The store sold 307 shirts and hats, so in this case it sold 307 − 89 = 218 hats. The earnings from the hats would be 218 × $5 = $1,090, for a total of $1,757.50 from both shirts and hats. That's not enough money, so eliminate (B). Sometimes, you might not be sure if you need a larger number or a smaller one. In that case, just pick a direction and see if you get closer to what you want. In order to make more money in this question, the store would need to sell more of the expensive item and fewer of the cheaper item, so try a larger number of shirts. If the store sold 115 shirts, the earnings would be $862.50. The store would sell 192 hats and earn $960 for a total of $1,822.50. This matches the target earnings, so (C) is correct.

Tips for Happiness when Plugging In the Answer Choices

- Choices (B) and (C) are good answers to start with; use whichever one is easiest to work with.

- The answers will be in numerical order, so you will often be able to eliminate answers that are either too big or too small, based on the result of the first choice you plug in. If the answer to (B) or (C) was too small, you should try bigger answer choices. If the answer was too big, try smaller answer choices.

- Don't try to work out all the steps in advance—the nice thing about plugging in is that you do the steps one at a time.

- Plugging In questions may be long word problems or short arithmetic problems, and they can be easy, medium, or hard. The more difficult the question, the better off you'll be plugging in.

- Make a chart if you have a lot of stuff to keep track of.

QUICK QUIZ #2

Easy

6

If 4 less than the product of b and 6 is 44, what is the value of b ?

A) 4

B) 6

C) 8

D) 14

Medium

13

A store reduces the price of a CD player by 20% and then reduces that price by 15%. If the final price of the CD player is $170, what was its original price?

A) $140

B) $185

C) $200

D) $250

Hard

24

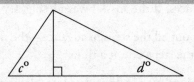

In the figure shown above, sin (*c*°) = cos (*d*°). If *c* = 3*y* – 27 and *d* = 7*y* – 16, what is the value of *y* ?

A) 3.3

B) 5.3

C) 10.3

D) 13.3

Answers and Explanations: Quick Quiz #2

6. **C** Try (B) first, so *b* = 6. The product of 6 and 6 is 36, and 4 less than 36 is 32. 32 isn't 44, so cross out (B). Try a higher number, (C). If *b* = 8, the product of 8 and 6 is 48, and 4 less than 48 is 44.

13. **D** Try (C) first. If the original price of the CD player was $200, then 20% of 200 is 40. That leaves us with a price of $160. Hey—the final price was $170, and you're already below that. You need a higher number. Try (D): If the original price was $250, take 20% of 250, which is 50. Now the price is $200. Take another 15% ($30) off and you get 200 – 30 = 170.

24. **D** This is a hard one that expects you to know some things about trigonometry. You may not recognize the rule being tested, but you should see the opportunity to use PITA. The answers represent *y*, so plug them into the equations for *c* and *d* and get those values. Then it's just a matter of using your calculator's handy SIN and COS buttons to see if sin (*c*°) = cos (*d*°). Start with (C): if *y* = 10.3, *c* = 3(10.3) – 27 = 3.9 and *d* = 7(10.3) – 16 = 56.1. Use your calculator, in degree mode, to find that sin (3.9°) = 0.068 and cos (65.1°) = 0.421. These aren't equal, so eliminate (C). It may be hard to tell which way to go, but at worst,

you'll have to try three of the four answers, which should still be worth the time. In this case, a smaller number will make c negative, which probably won't work, so go bigger. Now try (D): if $y = 13.3$, $c = 12.9$ and $d = 77.1$. Since sin (12.9°) = 0.223 and cos (77.1°) = 0.223, (D) is correct. You may notice how 12.9° and 77.1° add up to 90°. This question is really testing if you know that for the complementary angles in a right triangle, the sine of one is equal to the cosine of the other, and vice versa. Using PITA, though, you could avoid that entirely.

Do a little analysis. See how the questions got harder as you went along? For the easy question, you had to read carefully, multiply, and subtract. For the medium question, you had to take percentages. For the hard question, you had to deal with geometry and were confronted with a trigonometry rule that you might not have known. For all the questions, plugging in allowed you to avoid writing an equation or getting confused. Less work is good.

ESTIMATING

A Rough Estimate May Be All That's Necessary

The less work the better. Maybe you'll only be able to eliminate a couple of answers. That's okay too.

For example:

8

Chris can run 3.6 miles in 44 minutes. If he continues to run at this pace, which of the following is closest to the distance he will travel in 3 hours?

A)   5 miles

B)   10 miles

C)   15 miles

D)   20 miles

Solution: This question appears in the calculator section, so you could take the time to get an exact answer to it. However, the question asks for which answer is the "closest" to the actual value, and the choices are spread apart. These are clues that you can estimate. If Chris can run 3.6 miles in 44 minutes, he would go about another mile in another 15 minutes. So his speed is almost 5 miles per hour. In 3 hours, he would go about 15 miles, making (C) the most likely answer. (It's also the correct one!)

There are two advantages to solving the problem this way. First, you avoid having to do the last step of the problem and gain yourself some time. Second, you avoid even the possibility of making a careless mistake along the way.

We know you can probably find the "real" answer to this question. That's not the issue. On a timed test, with a lot of pressure on you, the fewer steps you have to do, the better off you are.

This is a fabulous piece of news—it means that you should use your eyes to estimate distances and angles, instead of jumping immediately to formulas and equations. You aren't allowed to bring a ruler or a protractor into the test. But you can often tell if one line is longer than another, or if the shaded part of a circle is larger than the unshaded part, just by estimating. That should allow you to eliminate at least a couple of answers, maybe more.

Is this a sketchy technique? Are we telling you to take the easy way out? No and yes. ETS and the College Board, the companies that write the SAT, doesn't mind if you use your common sense. Neither do we. And as for the easy way out…yes, that's exactly what you're training yourself to look for.

Estimating is not totally foreign to you. Think of geometry problems you encounter in real life—parking a car, packing a box, even shooting a basketball. We guess you don't take out a pad and pencil and start calculating to solve any of these problems. You estimate them, and see what happens.

Same deal on the SAT.

For example:

25

 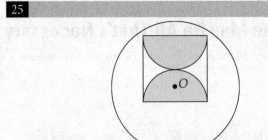

In the circle above with center O, the radius of the circle is equal to the length of a side of the square. If the shaded region represents two semicircles inscribed in the square, the ratio of the area of the shaded region to the area of the circle is

A) 1:16

B) 1:8

C) 1:4

D) 2:3

Solution: Look at the figure. How much of it looks shaded? Less than half? Sure. Cross out (D). If you're good at estimating, maybe you can cross out (A) as well. (Try drawing more semi-circles in the big circle and see how many will fit.) Now let's figure it out, using our good friend Plugging In: Let the radius = 2. So the area is 4π. If the radius = 2, the side of the square is 2. The shaded part consists of 2 semi-circles, each with a radius that's the side of the square, so the radius of the small circle is 1, and the area is π. Put the small area over the big area and you get $\dfrac{\pi}{4\pi}$, which is a ratio of 1:4.

QUICK QUIZ #3

Easy

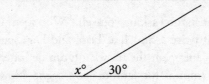

Which of the following is equal to 3x ?

A) 50

B) 150

C) 360

D) 450

Medium

Dan, Laura, and Jane went grocery shopping. Dan spent three times as much as Laura and half as much as Jane. If they spent a total of $50 on groceries, how much did Jane spend?

A) $15

B) $25

C) $30

D) $45

Hard

Three numbers, a, b, and c, have a sum of 672. The value of a is 25% less than the sum of b and c. What is the value of a ?

A) 97

B) 135

C) 288

D) 372

Answers and Explanations: Quick Quiz #3

4. **D** Angle x is pretty big, isn't it? So $3x$ is really, really big. Cross out (A). Now work it out: $x + 30 = 180$, so $x = 150$. And $3x = 450$. If you fail to estimate, you might forget to multiply by 3 and pick (B). You might fall asleep for a split second and divide by 3 and pick (A). Estimating protects you against such disasters.

13. **C** You might start by asking yourself, "Who spent the most money?" Since Jane spent twice as much as Dan, and Dan spent three times as much as Laura, Jane spent the most. You can definitely eliminate (A); it's too small an amount for Jane to have spent. Now Plug In the Answers. Begin with (B) or (C), since (A) is out. Which is the easier number to cut in half?

	J	D	L
(C)	30	15	5

$30 + $15 + $5 = $50, so (C) is the answer.

21. **C** Start by estimating. The value of a can't be too small, if it is close to the sum of b and c. Choice (A) is probably too small, so eliminate it. The value of a also can't be more than half the total, since it is less than the sum of the other two numbers. Therefore, (D) is too big. With only (B) and (C) left, you could just guess and go, but using PITA will get you the right answer. For (C), if $a = 288$, there is $672 - 288 = 384$ left for the sum of b and c. Is $288 = 384 - \dfrac{25}{100}(384)$? Yes, it is, so (C) is the correct answer.

Tips for Estimating Happiness

- With geometry, especially on hard questions, the answer choices need to be translated into numbers that you can work with.

- Translate π to a bit more than 3; $\sqrt{2}$ is 1.4; $\sqrt{3}$ is 1.7.

- Practice estimating *a lot*, even if you're going to work out the problem—and notice how your estimates improve.

- The farther apart the answer choices, the bigger the opportunity for eliminating answers by estimating.

- If the figure is NOT drawn to scale, redraw it if you can, using whatever measurements are provided. Then go ahead and estimate. If you can't redraw it, don't estimate.

- If two things look about equal, you can't assume that they're *exactly* equal.

- Trust what your eyes tell you.

How to Apply These Techniques

To study efficiently for the SAT, you must:

- Practice plugging in. Plug in whenever and wherever you can.

- Analyze your work so that you can avoid making the same mistakes over and over.

- Do the problems in this book as though you are taking the real thing—practice with the same focus and intensity you will need on the actual SAT.

Chapter 2
Arithmetic

Much of this chapter will be review, but study it well. Even though the SAT tests many basic mathematical concepts, these concepts are tested in very particular ways. To do well on the SAT requires that you know these definitions backward and forward.

After each section of review is a Quick Quiz with a variety of questions: easy, medium, and hard. If you get *all* of them right, you're in very good shape. And keep in mind: You could leave all the hard questions blank and still get a good score. So make sure you're getting the easy and medium ones right first.

DEFINITIONS

consecutive	numbers in order (1, 2, 3, etc.)
denominator	the bottom number of a fraction
difference	what you get when you subtract one number from another
digit	a number from 0 to 9. For example, 376 is a three-digit number.
distinct	different (i.e., the distinct factors of 4 are 1, 4, and 2—not 1, 4, 2, and 2)
even	a number evenly divisible by 2 (0 is even)
factor	same meaning as "division": a smaller number that goes into your number (example: 2 is a factor of 8)
multiple	a bigger number that your number goes into (example: 8 is a multiple of 2)
numerator	the top number of a fraction
odd	a number not evenly divisible by 2
PEMDAS	you won't see that written on the test—it's a handy acronym for the order of operations: Parentheses, Exponents, Multiplication, Division, Addition, Subtraction. Learn it, live it.
places	in 234.167, 2 is the hundreds place, 3 is the tens place, 4 is the ones or units digit, 1 is the tenths place, 6 is the hundredths place, and 7 is the thousandths place.
prime	a number divisible evenly only by itself and 1. The first five primes are 2, 3, 5, 7, and 11. (Note: 1 is not prime.)
product	what you get when you multiply two numbers together
quotient	what you get after dividing one number into another
reciprocal	whatever you multiply a number by to get 1 (i.e., the reciprocal of $\frac{1}{2}$ is $\frac{2}{1}$. The reciprocal of 6 is $\frac{1}{6}$.)
remainder	what's left over if a division problem doesn't work out evenly
sum	what you get when you add together two numbers

DIVISIBILITY

On the SAT, **divisible** means dividing evenly, with no remainder. This means that 16 is divisible by 4, but 18 is not divisible by 4. To figure out whether one number is divisible by another, one option may be to use your calculator. However, if you're working in the section in which there is no calculator allowed, you may have to rely on long division.

Long division may be something you haven't done in a while and may seem a little intimidating. However, if your younger self was able to master it, you can too! Let's look at an example. Is 120 divisible by 8? Try to divide.

$$8 \overline{)120}$$

Divide one digit at a time. Does 8 go into 1? No, because 8 is greater than 1. Does 8 go into 12? Not evenly, but it does go in one time.

$$\begin{array}{r} 1 \\ 8 \overline{)120} \end{array}$$

Multiply 8 by 1 and subtract it from 12.

$$\begin{array}{r} 1 \\ 8 \overline{)120} \\ -8 \\ \hline 4 \end{array}$$

Now go to the next digit. Carry down the 0 in 120 to the bottom to make 40.

$$\begin{array}{r} 1 \\ 8 \overline{)120} \\ -8 \\ \hline 40 \end{array}$$

Does 8 go into 40? Yes, it goes in 5 times. Put a 5 above the 0 and multiply 5 by 8 to get 40.

$$\begin{array}{r} 15 \\ 8 \overline{)120} \\ -8 \\ \hline 40 \\ -40 \\ \hline \end{array}$$

Subtract 40 from 40 to get 0. Because there is no remainder, 8 divides evenly into 120 and thus 120 is divisible by 8.

Let's look at another example. Is 8 divisible by 124? The long division will work similarly.

$$\begin{array}{r} 15 \\ 8 \overline{)124} \\ -8 \\ \hline 44 \\ -40 \\ \hline 4 \end{array}$$

One difference, however, is that the 4 from 124 is carried down rather than the 0 from 120. As a result, 40 is subtracted from 44 rather than from 40, so the remainder is no longer 0. Because the remainder isn't 0, 124 is not divisible by 8.

A possible alternative to long division is reducing fractions. Remember that the fraction bar is the same as the division sign, so $120 \div 8 = \dfrac{120}{8}$ and $124 \div 8 = \dfrac{124}{8}$. To determine whether 120 is divisible by 8, reduce the fraction $\dfrac{120}{8}$. Because both the numerator and the denominator are even, divide both by 2 to get $\dfrac{60}{4}$. Both the numerator and denominator are still even, so divide by 2 again to get $\dfrac{30}{2}$. This can be repeated yet again, to get $\dfrac{15}{1} = 15$. Because this fraction reduces to a whole number, $120 \div 8 = 15$ and 120 is divisible by 8. Similarly, reduce the fraction $\dfrac{124}{8}$ by 2 to get $\dfrac{62}{4}$ and by 2 again to get $\dfrac{31}{2}$. This cannot reduce further. Because $\dfrac{124}{8}$ does not reduce to a whole number, 124 is not divisible by 8.

Factoring shows up on the SAT all over the place. That's okay; it's easy.

To find all of the factors of a number, factor in pairs. Start with 1 and make a list of all the pairs that multiply together to equal the original number:

What are the factors of 36?

> 1, 36
> 2, 18
> 3, 12
> 4, 9
> 6, 6

To find the prime factors of a number, simply find all the factors as shown above, and then select only those that are also prime numbers.

QUICK QUIZ #1

Easy

> **2**
>
> Which of the following could be a factor of $n(n + 1)$, if n is a positive integer less than 3 ?
>
> A) 3
>
> B) 4
>
> C) 5
>
> D) 9

Medium

> **23**
>
> An art teacher has a jar containing b buttons to distribute to her class for a project. In order to give each child in the class 6 buttons, she will need 18 more buttons. If she gives each child 5 buttons, she will have 4 left over. How many children are in the class?
>
> A) 17
>
> B) 19
>
> C) 22
>
> D) 24

Answers and Explanations: Quick Quiz #1

2. **A**   Plug In. If $n = 1$, $1(1 + 1) = 2$. None of the answers are factors of 2. If $n = 2$, $2(2 + 1) = 6$. 3 is a factor of 6, so the answer is (A).

23. **C**   Plug In the Answers, starting with one of the middle ones. If there are 22 students in the class, the teacher will need $22 \times 6 = 132$ buttons in order to give each child 6 buttons. The question says she is 18 buttons short, so subtract 18 from 132 to find that $b = 114$ buttons. In the second scenario, she has 4 buttons left over, so subtract 4 to get 110. Is that divisible by 5 to give 5 buttons to each child? Yes! 110 divided by 5 is 22, the number of children in the class. So (C) works and is the correct answer.

FRACTIONS

To add fractions, get a common denominator and then add across the top:

$$\frac{1}{2}+\frac{2}{3}=\frac{3}{6}+\frac{4}{6}=\frac{7}{6} \qquad \frac{1}{x}+\frac{2}{x+2}=\frac{(x+2)}{x(x+2)}+\frac{(x\cdot2)}{x(x+2)}=\frac{3x+2}{x^2+2x}$$

To subtract fractions, it's the same deal, but subtract across the top:

$$\frac{3}{4}-\frac{1}{3}=\frac{9}{12}-\frac{4}{12}=\frac{5}{12} \qquad \frac{2}{x^2}-\frac{1}{xy}=\frac{2\cdot y}{x^2\cdot y}-\frac{x}{x\cdot xy}=\frac{2y-x}{x^2y}$$

To multiply fractions, cancel if you can, then multiply across, top and bottom:

$$\frac{1}{2}\cdot\frac{3}{5}=\frac{3}{10} \qquad \frac{2}{\cancel{7}_1}\cdot\frac{\cancel{14}^2}{9}=\frac{4}{9} \qquad \frac{x}{\cancel{x-1}}\cdot\frac{x\cancel{(x-1)}}{x^2+2}=\frac{x^2}{x^2+2}$$

To divide fractions, flip the second one, then multiply across, top and bottom:

$$\frac{2}{3}\div\frac{1}{2}=\frac{2}{3}\cdot\frac{2}{1}=\frac{4}{3} \qquad \frac{3x}{1-x}\div\frac{1+x}{x}=\frac{3x}{1-x}\cdot\frac{x}{1+x}=\frac{3x^2}{1-x^2}$$

To see which of the two fractions is bigger, cross-multiply from bottom to top. The side with the bigger product is the bigger fraction.

$$55\swarrow\frac{5}{7}\diagup\frac{8}{11}\searrow56$$

56 is bigger than 55, so $\frac{8}{11}$ is bigger.

QUICK QUIZ #2

Easy

18

If $\dfrac{9}{10}y - \dfrac{7}{10}y = \dfrac{4}{3} - \dfrac{8}{15}$, what is the value of y ?

Medium

21

In a jar of cookies, there is $\dfrac{1}{6}$ probability of randomly selecting an oatmeal-raisin cookie and a $\dfrac{1}{8}$ probability of selecting a sugar cookie. If the remaining cookies are all chocolate chip cookies, then which one of the following could be the number of cookies in the jar?

A) 16

B) 20

C) 24

D) 32

Hard

28

At a track meet, $\frac{2}{5}$ of the first-place finishers attended Southport High School, and $\frac{1}{2}$ of them were girls. If $\frac{2}{9}$ of the first-place finishers who did NOT attend Southport High School were girls, what fractional part of the total number of first-place finishers were boys?

A) $\frac{1}{9}$

B) $\frac{2}{15}$

C) $\frac{3}{5}$

D) $\frac{2}{3}$

Answers and Explanations: Quick Quiz #2

18. **4** Since the fractions on the left have a common denominator, start there. Subtract across the top to get $\frac{2}{10}y$, which can be reduced to $\frac{1}{5}y$. Now get a common denominator on the right by multiplying $\frac{4}{3}$ by $\frac{5}{5}$. This becomes $\frac{20}{15}$, and now you can subtract across the top on the right to get $\frac{12}{15}$. The full equation is now $\frac{1}{5}y = \frac{12}{15}$. Multiply both sides by 5 to get $y = \frac{12}{15} \cdot 5 = \frac{12}{3} = 4$. Grid that into the box.

21. **C** Plug In the Answers. Start with one of the middle choices, such as (B). If there are 20 cookies in the jar, how many oatmeal-raisin cookies are there? Not a whole number, so this can't be correct. While it is not clear whether you need a bigger or smaller number, you now see that you need a number that is divisible by both six and eight, so both fractions will yield a whole number. Choice (A) is 16, which is divisible by 8 but not by 6. Eliminate (A). Choice (C) is 24, which is divisible by both 6 and 8. Keep (C). Choice (D) is 32, which is divisible by 8 but not by 6. Eliminate (D). The correct answer is (C).

28.   **D**   Plug In. The total number of first-place finishers was 30. You can find the number who were from Southport by taking $\frac{2}{5}$ of 30 = 12. That leaves 18 who did not go to Southport High School. If half the 12 Southport runners were girls, that means 6 were girls and 6 were boys. If $\frac{2}{9}$ of the non-Southport runners were girls, then $\frac{2}{9}$ of 18 = 4 girls, which leaves 14 boys. That means a total of 14 + 6 = 20 boys, out of a total of 30, or $\frac{20}{30} = \frac{2}{3}$. You will be happier if you make a tree chart:

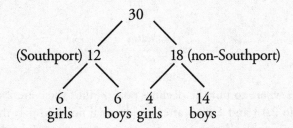

DECIMALS

To add, subtract, multiply, or divide decimals, the easiest way is use your calculator. Remember to check each number as you punch it in, and be extra careful with the decimal point. However, on the non-calculator section, you'll need to know how to do it by hand.

Addition and subtraction use the same method. Stack the two numbers with the decimal points lined up. Then add or subtract as you normally would. For example, to add 12.2 + 5.91, line it up like this:

$$\begin{array}{r} 12.20 \\ + \ 5.91 \\ \hline \end{array}$$

Notice that a 0 is added to the end of 12.2 to help the number align properly. Now carry down the decimal point and add the numbers to get

$$\begin{array}{r} \overset{1}{1}2.20 \\ + \ 5.91 \\ \hline 18.11 \end{array}$$

Subtraction works the same way. For example, to subtract 4.8 from 7.94, line it up to get

$$\begin{array}{r} 7.94 \\ - \ 4.80 \\ \hline \end{array}$$

Then bring down the decimal and subtract to get

$$\begin{array}{r} 7.94 \\ - \ 4.80 \\ \hline 3.14 \end{array}$$

To multiply, start by ignoring the decimals and multiplying as if the terms were whole numbers. Then count the total number of decimal places in the two numbers combined. That is the number of places that should be after the decimal point in the answer. For example, to multiply 2.13 by 3.1, set up

$$\begin{array}{r} 2.13 \\ \times\ 3.1 \end{array}$$

There is no need to line up the decimal points in the case of multiplication, because the decimal points are ignored in the first step. Proceed as if you're multiplying 213 by 31 to get

$$\begin{array}{r} 2.13 \\ \times\ 3.1 \\ \hline 213 \\ +\ 6390 \\ \hline 6603 \end{array}$$

Now determine where to put the decimal point. Since there are 2 digits after the decimal point in 2.13 and 1 digit after the decimal point in 3.1, there have to be 2 + 1 = 3 digits after the decimal point in the answer. Therefore, the final answer is 6.603.

$$\begin{array}{r} 2.13 \\ \times\ 3.1 \\ \hline 213 \\ +\ 6390 \\ \hline 6.603 \end{array}$$

To divide decimals, use long division. For example, let's do 7.15 ÷ 2.2 Begin by setting up normal long division.

$$2.2\overline{)7.15}$$

You don't want to deal with a decimal on the outside, so move the decimal to the right by 1. To compensate for this, do the same to the number on the inside to get

$$22\overline{)71.5}$$

Now, carry up the decimal to get

$$22\overline{)71.5}^{\,.}$$

Now proceed with long division as if the decimal is not there. 22 goes into 71 three times, so

$$22\overline{)71.5}^{\,3.}$$

Multiply 22 by 3 to get 66. Subtract 66 from 71 to get 5. Carry down the 5 to get

$$\begin{array}{r} 3. \\ 22\overline{)71.5} \\ -\ 66 \\ \hline 55 \end{array}$$

22 goes into 55 twice. Multiply 22 by 2 to get 44. Subtract 44 from 55 to get 11.

$$
\begin{array}{r}
3.2 \\
22\overline{\smash{)}71.5} \\
-66 \\
\hline
55 \\
-44 \\
\hline
11
\end{array}
$$

There is 11 left over. To handle this, add a 0 to the end of 71.5 and carry down the 0.

$$
\begin{array}{r}
3.2 \\
22\overline{\smash{)}71.50} \\
-66 \\
\hline
55 \\
-44 \\
\hline
110
\end{array}
$$

Now, 22 goes into 110 five times. Multiply 22 by 5 to get 110. Subtract 110 from 110 to get 0.

$$
\begin{array}{r}
3.25 \\
22\overline{\smash{)}71.50} \\
-66 \\
\hline
55 \\
-44 \\
\hline
110 \\
-110 \\
\hline
0
\end{array}
$$

Since the remainder is 0, the division is complete and $7.15 \div 2.2 = 3.25$.

To convert a fraction to a decimal, divide the numerator by the denominator:

$$\frac{1}{2} = 1 \div 2 = 0.5 \qquad \frac{5}{8} = 5 \div 8 = 0.625 \qquad \frac{4}{3} = 4 \div 3 = 1.3\overline{33}$$

To convert a decimal to a fraction, count up the number of digits to the right of the decimal point and put that many zeros in your denominator:

$$0.2 = \frac{2}{10} \qquad 0.314 = \frac{314}{1,000} \qquad 2.23 = \frac{223}{100}$$

QUICK QUIZ #3

Easy

1

If $0.2p = 4$, what is the value of $4p$?

A) 2

B) 8

C) 40

D) 80

Medium

15

For positive integers y and z, if $z^2 = y^3$ and $y^2 = 16$, what is the value of $\dfrac{y}{z}$?

A) 0.5

B) 0.4

C) 0.2

D) 2

Hard

29

For all values of a, b, c, and d, which of the following

is equivalent to $\dfrac{\dfrac{ad}{bc}}{\dfrac{ac}{bd}}$?

A) a^2c^2

B) $\dfrac{a^2}{b^2}$

C) $\dfrac{d^2}{c^2}$

D) b^2d^2

Answers and Explanations: Quick Quiz #3

1. **D** If $0.2p = 4$, then divide both sides by 0.2 to get $p = 20$. Then, multiply both sides by 4 to get $4p = 80$.

15. **A** If $y^2 = 16$, then $y = 4$. If $z^2 = y^3$, then $z^2 = 64$ and $z = 8$.

    So $\dfrac{y}{z} = \dfrac{4}{8} = \dfrac{1}{2} = 0.5$.

29. **C** Remember that to divide fractions, you flip the denominator and multiply. (Dividing is the same as multiplying by the reciprocal.)

    So $\dfrac{\dfrac{ad}{bc}}{\dfrac{ac}{bd}} = \dfrac{ad}{bc} \cdot \dfrac{bd}{ac} = \dfrac{a\,bd^2}{abc^2} = \dfrac{d^2}{c^2}$.

PERCENTAGES

For some reason, many people get hung up on percents, probably because they are trying to remember a series of operations rather than using their common sense.

A percentage is simply a fractional part—50% of something is one-half of something, and 47% is a little less than half. It is very helpful to approximate percents in this way, and not to think of them as abstract, meaningless numbers. 3.34% is very little of something, 0.0012% a tiny part of something, and 105% a little more than the whole.

Keep in mind that since percents are an expression of the fractional part, they do not represent actual numbers. If, for example, you're a salesperson, and you earn a 15% commission on what you sell, you'll get a lot richer selling Rolls-Royces than you will selling doughnuts. Even thousands of doughnuts. All examples of 15% are not created equal, unless they are 15% of the same number.

Now for the nitty-gritty:

To convert a percent to a decimal, move the decimal point two spaces to the left:

$$50\% = 0.5 \qquad 4\% = 0.04 \qquad 0.03\% = 0.0003 \qquad 112\% = 1.12$$

To convert a decimal to a percent, move the decimal point two spaces to the right:

$$0.5 = 50\% \qquad 0.66 = 66\% \qquad 0.01 = 1\% \qquad 4 = 400\%$$

To convert a percent to a fraction, put the number over 100:

$$50\% = \frac{50}{100} \qquad 4\% = \frac{4}{100} \qquad 106\% = \frac{106}{100} \qquad x = \frac{x}{100}$$

To get a percent of a number, multiply by the decimal. For example, to get 22% of 50, first change the percentage to a decimal by moving the decimal point two places to the left = 0.22. Then multiply on your calculator.

If no calculator is allowed, it may be easier to use fractions. In this case, to get 22% of 50,

$$\frac{22}{100} \cdot 50 = \frac{22}{100} \cdot \frac{50}{1} = \frac{22}{\cancel{100}_{2}} \cdot \frac{\cancel{50}^{1}}{1} = \frac{22}{2} = 11$$

The second way to get a percent of a number is to translate your sentence into an equation. This is easier than it sounds. Convert the percent to a fraction and substitute $\times$ for *of*, = for *is*, and x for *what*.

What is 50% of 16?

This question translates to $x = \frac{50}{100} \times 16$.

This method is particularly useful for complicated percents:

What is 10% of 40% of 22?

This question translates to $x = \frac{10}{100} \times \frac{40}{100} \times 22$.

To calculate what percent one number is of another number, use the translation method, substituting $\frac{x}{100}$ for what percent.

What percent of 16 is 8?

This question translates to $\frac{x}{100} \times 16 = 8$.

8 is what percent of 16?

This question translates to $8 = \frac{x}{100} \times 16$.

Notice that even though these equations look a little different, they will produce the same answer.

QUICK QUIZ #4

Easy

3

If 20% of p is 10, what is 10% of p ?

A) 2

B) 4

C) 5

D) 8

Medium

Mabel agreed to pay the tax and tip for dinner at a restaurant with her four friends. Each of the friends paid an equal part of the cost of the dinner, which was $96. If the tax and tip together were 20% of the cost of the meal, Mabel paid how much less than any one of her friends?

A) $2.40

B) $4.80

C) $19.20

D) $24.00

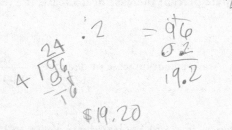

Hard

28

If 200% of 40% of x is equal to 40% of y, then x is what percent of y?

A) 10%

B) 20%

C) 50%

D) 80%

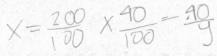

Answers and Explanations: Quick Quiz #4

3. **C** The question asks for 10% of p and gives 20% of p. Because 10% is half of 20%, cut the value of 20% of p (10) by half (5). You could also have solved this problem by solving for p. To do so, translate the sentence: $\frac{20}{100} \times p = 10$. $\frac{p}{5} = 10$, and $p = 50$. Now do the next step: $0.1 \times 50 = 5$.

11. **B** First, calculate what each friend paid: $96 \div 4 = \$24$. Now do the percentage: $0.20 \times 96 = \$19.20$. Subtract the second number from the first. If you noticed that each of the four friends paid 25%, and Mabel paid 20%, you could take a fast shortcut by taking the difference, or 5% of 96. [If you picked (C) or (D), you should reread the question before picking your final answer.]

28. **C**   Plug in 100 = *x*. 40% of 100 is 40, and 200% of 40 is 2 × 40 = 80. Now the question says that 80 is 40% of *y*, so *y* = 200, and (80 = 0.4*y*).

The question asks "*x* is what percent of *y*?," which you can write out as $100 = \frac{p}{100} \times 200$. Or you can simply realize that 100 is half of 200, which is 50%.

More on Percentages

To calculate percent increase or decrease, use the following formula:

$$\text{percent increase or decrease} = \frac{\text{difference}}{\text{original amount}} \times 100$$

For instance, if a $40 book was reduced to $35, the difference in price is $5. Therefore, the percent decrease is equal to $\frac{5}{40} \times 100$, which is the same as × 100, or 12.5%.

CHARTS AND GRAPHS

Many questions about percents and other arithmetic topics will involve charts and graphs. The key to these questions is to take a moment to size up the data before you attack the question. Pay particular attention to what units are used.

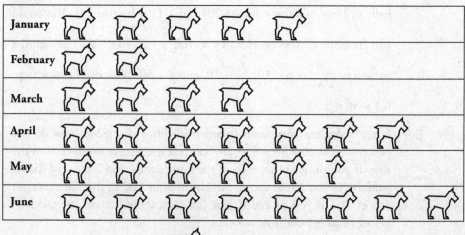

Number of Dogs Washed by Deidre's Dog Wash

 = 100 dogs

Above is a chart representing how many dogs were washed by Deirdre's Dog Wash in the first half of 2004. Which month features the greatest percent increase of the number of dogs washed over the previous month?

A) February

B) March

C) April

D) June

First, note the units. Each dog shape represents 100 dogs. Now, attack the question. You need to find the percent increase, which you'll recall is the difference between two numbers divided by the original number. Choice (A) shows a decrease in the number of dogs, so eliminate it. In March, 400 dogs were washed, while 200 dogs were washed in the previous month. Using the percent increase formula, we get

$$\frac{\text{difference}}{\text{original}} = \frac{400 - 200}{200} = \frac{200}{200} = 100\%$$

None of the other choices is even close, so (B) is our answer.

QUICK QUIZ #5

Medium

6

Adore-a-Bubble Soda Company's Sales

Flavor	1980	2000
Snappy Apple	50%	50%
Raspberry Rush	25%	5%
Fresh Fizz	10%	12%
Cranberry Crackle	12%	10%
Purple Pop	3%	3%
Total	100%	100%

The table above shows the Adore-a-Bubble Soda Company's sales for 1980 and 2000. The company sold 200 trillion cans of soda in 1980. If the company sold 40 trillion more cans of soda in 2000 than it did in 1980, then for which flavor did the <u>number</u> of cans of soda sold increase by 20% from 1980 to 2000 ?

A) Snappy Apple

B) Raspberry Rush

C) Fresh Fizz

D) Cranberry Crackle

14

A store owner buys a pound of grapes for 80 cents and sells it for a dollar. What percent of the selling price of grapes is the store owner's profit?

A) 20%

B) 25%

C) 40%

D) 80%

Hard

27

On the first test of the semester, Barbara scored a 60. On the last test of the semester, Barbara scored a 75. By what percent did Barbara's score improve?

A) 15%

B) 18%

C) 20%

D) 25%

Answers and Explanations: Quick Quiz #5

6. **A**   Use percent translation and the percent increase/decrease formula. For example, the number of cans of Snappy Apple sold in 1980 is 50% of 200 trillion. Using translation, you get $\frac{50}{100} \times 200$ trillion $= \frac{1}{2} \times 200$ trillion = 100 trillion. In 2000, the company sold 50% of 240 trillion. Using translation again gives you 120 trillion. Now you need to find the percent increase using the formula:

$$\text{percent increase} = \frac{\text{difference}}{\text{original}} \times 100$$

Plugging in the values you found above gives you $\frac{120 \text{ trillion} - 100 \text{ trillion}}{100 \text{ trillion}} \times 100 = \frac{1}{5} \times 100 = 20$. This means that sales of Snappy Apple increased by 20%, so (A) is the correct answer.

14. **A**   First, determine the store owner's profit. Change everything to cents so that you're only working with one unit: 100 − 80 = 20. Now translate the question into math terms: $\frac{x}{100} \cdot 100 = 20$.

27. **D**   Find the difference: 75 − 60 = 15. Put this difference (15) over the lower number: $\frac{15}{60}$. Reduce the fraction to $\frac{1}{4}$, which is 25%. Or divide it on your calculator, which will give you 0.25. Convert it to a percentage by moving the decimal two places to the right.

> Estimating is always a good idea when you're doing a percentage question—often there are silly answers that you can cross out before you do any math at all.

RATIOS

A ratio is like a percentage—it tells you how much you have of one thing compared to how much you have of another thing. For example, if you have hats and T-shirts in a ratio of 2:3, then for every two hats, you have three T-shirts. What we don't know is the actual number of each. It could be two hats and three T-shirts. Or it could be four hats and six T-shirts. Or 20 hats and 30 T-shirts.

A ratio describes a relationship, not a total number.

Whenever you need to convert from a ratio in its most reduced form to real-life numbers, there are two key steps:

- Always add the ratio numbers to get a whole.

- Find the factor that connects a ratio number to its real-life counterpart. All of the ratio numbers get multiplied by this factor to convert to real-life numbers.

A great way to see those two steps in action is to use a Ratio Box.

In Mr. Peterson's class of 48 students, the ratio of boys to girls is 3:5.

Boys	Girls	Whole
3 +	5 =	8	← Ratio
×	×	×	← Multiply by
=	=	=	
		6	
=	=	=	
(18) +	30 =	48	← Actual number

i.   How many girls are in the class? _____30_____

ii.   How many boys are in the class? _____18_____

iii. Boys make up what fractional part of the class? __3/8__

iv.   If you answered $\frac{18}{48}$ above, what does that reduce to? ___3/8___

> Don't get the order of the ratio mixed up—if the problem says red marbles and blue marbles in a ratio of 1:2, the first number represents the red marbles and the second number represents the blue marbles.

QUICK QUIZ #6

Medium

12

If $\dfrac{x}{y} = \dfrac{4}{3}$ and $\dfrac{x}{k} = \dfrac{1}{2}$, what is the value of $\dfrac{k}{y}$?

A) $\dfrac{3}{8}$

B) $\dfrac{2}{3}$

C) $\dfrac{3}{2}$

D) $\dfrac{8}{3}$

16

The junior class at Mooreland High is composed of boys and girls in a ratio of 5:1. All of the following could be the number of students in the junior class EXCEPT

A) 24

B) 42

C) 54

D) 62

Hard

20

In a certain ocean region, the ratio of sharks to tuna to damselfish to guppies is 1 to 3 to 5 to 6. If there are 1,500 total fish in that region, how many of the fish are sharks?

A) 15

B) 100

C) 150

D) 450

Answers and Explanations: Quick Quiz #6

12. **D**   Since $x = 4$ in one ratio and $x = 1$ in the other, you can't compare them. First, make them equal. If you multiply the second ratio by $\frac{4}{4}$, you get $\frac{4}{8}$. (Notice that if you multiply all parts of the ratio by the same number, it doesn't change. It just takes an unreduced form.) Now the x's are the same in both ratios, so you can compare them, and $\frac{k}{y} = \frac{8}{3}$. You could also plug in, which would work at least as well.

16. **D**   If the ratio is 5:1, you can add the parts and get 6 students. Therefore, the number of students in the class must be a multiple of 6. All of the choices are multiples of 6 except (D).

20. **B**   Make the Ratio Box. There are always three rows: ratio, multiply by, and actual. Here, the columns are: sharks, tuna, damselfish, guppies, and Total. In the first row, enter the ratio numbers: 1, 3, 5, and 6. Add them up, and put the sum (15) under Total. As the actual total is 1,500, enter that number in the lower, right cell. What times 15 is 1,500? 100. So, enter 100 in all of the multiply by cells. You can solve for all four fish types by multiplying the ratio number by 100, or just solve for sharks, as that is the question.

PROPORTIONS

To set up a proportion, match categories on top and bottom. For example:

> If 10 nails cost 4 cents, how much do 50 nails cost?

$$\begin{matrix} \text{(nails)} \\ \text{(cents)} \end{matrix} \quad \frac{10}{4} = \frac{50}{x}$$

$$10x = 200, \text{ so } x = 20 \text{ cents}$$

The great thing about proportions is that it doesn't matter which is on top—if you match nails to nails and cents to cents (or whatever), you'll get the right answer. Be consistent.

To solve an **inverse variation** problem, use the following set-up.

$$x_1 y_1 = x_2 y_2$$

If the value of x is inversely proportional to the value of y and $y = 4$ when $x = 15$, what is the value of x when y is 12?

$$x(12) = (15)(4)$$

$$x = 5$$

To solve rate problems, set up a proportion:

> If Bonzo rode his unicycle 30 miles in 5 hours, how long would it take him to ride 12 miles at the same rate?

$$\text{(miles)} \quad \frac{30}{5} = \frac{12}{x} \quad \text{(hours)}$$

$$30x = 60$$

$$x = 2 \text{ hours}$$

Harder questions may require extra work by requiring unit conversions: hours to minutes, miles to feet, etc. Be on the lookout for shifts in units within the problem.

> If Bonzo rode his unicycle 2,640 feet in 5 minutes, what is his speed in miles per hour? (1 mile = 5,280 feet)

$$\text{(feet)} \quad \frac{2,640}{5} = \frac{x}{60} \quad \text{(minutes)}$$

$$5x = 158,400$$

$$x = 31,680 \text{ feet per hour}$$

$$\text{(feet)} \quad \frac{5,280}{1} = \frac{31,680}{x} \quad \text{(miles)}$$

$$5,280x = 31,680$$

$$x = 6 \text{ miles per hour}$$

QUICK QUIZ #7

Easy

| 2 |

Laura can solve 6 math questions in 12 minutes. Working at the same rate, how many minutes would it take Laura to solve 5 math questions?

A) 6

B) 9

C) 10

D) 11

$$\frac{6}{12} = \frac{5}{x}$$ 10

60

Medium

| 12 |

The length of time in hours that a certain battery will last is inversely proportional to the length of time in years that the battery spends in storage. If the battery spends 3 years in storage, it will last 25 hours, so how long must the battery have been in storage if it will last 15 hours?

A) 1.75 years

B) 5 years

C) $41\frac{2}{3}$ years

D) 75 years

$x_1 y_1 = x_2 y_2$

3 25 · 15

$3 \times 25 = x_2 \times 15$

$\frac{75}{15} = x_2 = 5$ years

Hard

| 26 |

A factory produced 15 trucks of the same model. If the trucks had a combined weight of $34\frac{1}{2}$ tons, how much, in pounds, did one of the trucks weigh?

(One ton = 2,000 pounds)

A) 2,200

B) 4,500

C) 4,600

D) 5,400

$15 = 34\frac{1}{2}$

$15 \overline{)34\frac{1}{2}}$ 2.3

2.3
$15 \overline{)34.5}$
30
45
0

2,30

2.   **C** $\dfrac{6}{12} = \dfrac{5}{x}$. Cross-multiply to get $6x = 60$ and $x = 10$.

12.   **B**   To do this problem, it is important to know the formula for inverse variation: $x_1 y_1 = x_2 y_2$. In this case, the x_1 is 3 years, y_1 is 25 hours, and y_2 is 15 hours. So set up the equation as follows: $3 \times 25 = x_2 \times 15$. $\dfrac{75}{15} = x_2 = 5$ years.

26.   **C**   You can do this two ways: You can convert from tons to pounds first or do it later. If you do it first, multiply $34.5 \times 2{,}000$. That gives you 69,000. Your proportion should look like this: $\dfrac{15}{69{,}000} = \dfrac{1}{x}$. So $15x_1 = 69{,}000$ and $x = 4{,}600$. Or you can divide 15 into 34.5, which gives you 2.3 tons per truck. Then multiply 2.3 times 2,000.

AVERAGES

You already know how to figure out an average. You can figure out your GPA, right?

To get the average (arithmetic mean) of a set of numbers, add them up, then divide by the number of things in the set:

What's the average of 3, 5, and 10? $3 + 5 + 10 = 18$ and $18 \div 3 = 6$.

Most of the time on the SAT you are not given a set of numbers and asked for the average—they want to make their questions a little harder than that. There are three elements at work here: the sum of the numbers, the number of things in the set, and the average. To get any of these elements, you need to know the other two.

The easy way to remember these relationships is by memorizing the "Average Pie."

Here's a glimpse of what that looks like:

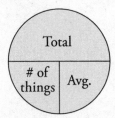

The *total* is the sum of all the numbers you're averaging, and the *number of things* is the number of elements you're averaging. Here's what the Average Pie looks like using the simple average example we just gave you.

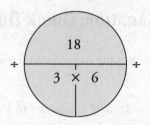

Here's how the Average Pie works mathematically. The horizontal line in the middle means *divide*. If you know the total and the number of things, just divide to get the average (18 ÷ 3 = 6). The vertical line means *multiply*. Thus if you know the total and the average, just divide to get the number of things (18 ÷ 6 = 3). If you know the average and the number of things, simply multiply to get the total (6 × 3 = 18). The key to most average questions is finding the total.

Here's another simple example:

Problem: If the average of three test scores is 70, what is the total of all three test scores?

Solution: Just put the number of things (3 tests) and the average (70) in the pie. Then multiply to find the total, which is 210.

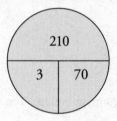

QUICK QUIZ #8

Easy

6

The average of 3 numbers is 22, and the smallest of these numbers is 2. What is the value of the other two numbers if they are equal?

A) 22
B) 30
C) 32
D) 64

Medium

17

Caroline scored 85, 88, and 89 on three of her four history tests. If her average score for all tests was 90, what did she score on her fourth test?

A) 90
B) 93
C) 96
D) 98

Hard

24

The average of 8, 13, x, and y is 6. The average of 15, 9, x, and x is 8. What is the value of y ?

A) −1
B) 0
C) 4
D) 6

Answers and Explanations: Quick Quiz #8

6. **C** If the average of 3 numbers is 22, then their sum is 3×22 or 66. Take away the 2 and you've got 64 left. If the other two numbers are equal, divide 64 by 2 = 32.

17. **D** Caroline's final average was 90 on 4 tests. Therefore, you can use the Average Pie to figure out the total number of points she had on those four tests, by multiplying $90 \times 4 = 360$. You also know her scores on the first three tests, so if you subtract $360 - 85 - 88 - 89$, you get 98 points, which is the total score she must have gotten on her fourth test.

24. **A** Since the average of 8, 13, x, and y is 6, you know that their total must be equal to 6×4 or 24. This means that $8 + 13 + x + y = 24$. If you subtract the 8 and the 13, you find that $x + y = 3$. You also know that the average of 15, 9, x, and x is 8, so their total must be equal to 32. $15 + 9 + x + x = 32$, so $x + x$ must equal 8, and $x = 4$. Since you know from earlier that $x + y = 3$, $y = -1$.

MEDIAN, MODE, SET, AND RANGE

Each of these terms involves finding a value or values in sets of numbers. A **set** is just a fancy term for a list of numbers.

One common type of set question involves median.

To find the median, first put the group of numbers in ascending order. If the group has an odd number of elements, the median is the middle number.

   set: 1, 4, 9, 18, 54   median: 9

   set: 2, 4, 4, 4, 5   median: 4

If the group has an even number of elements, the median is *the average (arithmetic mean)* of the two middle numbers.

   set: 3, 15, 17, 74   median: 16

   set: 1, 6, 7, 8   median: 6.5

The remaining types of set questions are quite rare:

To find the mode, just look to see which number in the group appears the most often.

   set: 1, 1, 3, 5, 3, 4, 22, 3, 6   mode: 3

   set: 2, 5, 9, 11, 11, 15, 22   mode: 11

To find the range, subtract the smallest number from the largest.

   set: 3, 15, 28, 33, 33, 33, 42   range: 39

QUICK QUIZ #9

Easy

6

Set *Q*: {10, 2, 3, 5, 1, 7, 5, 2} — put in order

If the smallest and largest numbers in Set *Q* are removed, what is the median of Set *Q* ?

A) 3.5

B) 4

C) 5

D) 6

Medium

12

High Temperatures

Temperature	Number of days
22	2
25	2
28	3
31	0
34	4
37	1
40	2

Janet recorded the number of days certain high temperatures were reached over a 14-day period. She later decided to add data for one more day. If the high temperature on that day was 37, what is the median temperature for the set of days?

A) 26.5

B) 28

C) 31

D) 34

Hard

28

If a set of 9 randomly selected numbers is generated, which one of the following changes CANNOT affect the value of the median?

A) Subtracting 2 from each number

B) Decreasing the largest number only

C) Decreasing the smallest number only

D) Increasing the largest and smallest numbers only

Answers and Explanations: Quick Quiz #9

6. **B**   Take out 10 and 1. Now write down the numbers in order: 2, 2, 3, 5, 5, 7. The middle of the list falls between 3 and 5, so the median is 4.

12. **D**   On a median question, it is essential to list out all of the numbers in order, including all of the repeated numbers. The original list of numbers, in order, is:

22, 22, 25, 25, 28, 28, 28, 34, 34, 34, 34, 37, 40, 40

Once the new number is added, the set of numbers is:

22, 22, 25, 25, 28, 28, 28, 34, 34, 34, 34, 37, 37, 40, 40

The middle number of the new list is 34. If you picked (C), you chose the original median.

28. **C**   Write out any set of nine numbers, such as 1 through 9. The median is 5. If you subtract 2 from each number, the median changes to 3, so (A) is wrong. If you decrease the largest number to 4 or less, the median will change to 4, so (B) is wrong. On the other hand, no matter how much you decrease the smallest number, the median will remain the same, so (C) is correct. Choice (D) is wrong because increasing the smallest number to 6 or more will change the median.

EXPONENTS AND ROOTS

An exponent tells you how many times to multiply a number by itself. So x^3 is really shorthand for $x \cdot x \cdot x$. If you have a momentary lapse and can't remember the following rules, it may help to write out your problem the long way and work from there.

For exponents with the same base, remember MADSPM:

To Multiply, Add the exponents: $x^2 \cdot x^5 = x^{2+5} = x^7$.

To Divide, Subtract the exponents: $x^6 \div x^3 = x^{6-3} = x^3$.

To raise the Power, Multiply: $(x^4)^3 = x^{4 \times 3} = x^{12}$.

You cannot add or subtract different exponents, so $x^6 + x^3$ is just $x^6 + x^3$. You can't simplify it.

For exponents with different bases:

The trick is to try to rewrite the numbers in terms of the same base. For example:

$$6^2 \times 12^4$$

becomes

$$6^2 \times (6 \times 2)^4 = 6^2 \times 6^4 \times 2^4$$

Now you can combine terms with the same base as above.

To deal with exponents and parentheses, remember that the exponent carries over to all parts within the parentheses:

$$2(3a^3)^2 = 2[(3^2)(a^6)] = 2(9a^6) = 18a^6$$

Keep in mind that 1 raised to any power is still just 1. ($1^{357} = 1$.)

Negative numbers with even exponents are positive; negative numbers with odd exponents are negative. Fractions with exponents get smaller, not bigger.

A **square root** is just a backward exponent; in other words, the number under the $\sqrt{}$ is what you get when you raise a number to a power of 2.

$$\sqrt{4} = 2 \qquad \sqrt{36} = 6 \qquad \sqrt{1} = 1$$

To multiply or divide square roots, combine the numbers under one root sign and then multiply or divide as usual.

$$\sqrt{7} \cdot \sqrt{3} = \sqrt{21} \qquad \sqrt{15} \div \sqrt{3} = \sqrt{5}$$

To add or subtract square roots, first make sure you have the same number under the $\sqrt{}$. Then add or subtract the number outside of the $\sqrt{}$.

$$5\sqrt{3} + 2\sqrt{3} = 7\sqrt{3} \qquad 6\sqrt{2} - \sqrt{2} = 5\sqrt{2}$$

Note that:

- A square root multiplied by itself is just that number without the $\sqrt{}$. $\sqrt{3} \cdot \sqrt{3} = 3$

- The square root of a fraction between 0 and 1 gets bigger. For example, $\sqrt{\dfrac{1}{4}} = \dfrac{\sqrt{1}}{\sqrt{4}} = \dfrac{1}{2}$.

- The square root of a number is always positive (on the SAT, anyway).

- The square root of 1 is 1.

Rational exponents combine powers with roots. To simplify the following expression:

$$8^{\frac{2}{3}}$$

First, we raise the base to the power of the numerator of the fraction. In this case, the numerator is two, so we'll square the base and get the following:

$$8^2 = 64$$

Now we'll deal with the denominator of the fraction. The denominator tells us what root to take the number to. In this case, the denominator is three, so we'll find the third root and end up with the following:

$$\sqrt[3]{64} = 4$$

QUICK QUIZ #10

Easy

1

If $(3x)^2 = 81$, which of the following is a possible value of x?

A) 2

B) 3

C) 6

D) 9

Medium

13

If $2a + b = 8$, what is the value of $9^a 3^b$?

A) The value cannot be determined from the information given.

B) 3^8

C) 9^3

D) 27^4

Hard

18

Which one of the following must be greater than x, if x is a real number?

A) $\dfrac{x}{4}$

B) $4x$

C) $x^2 + 1$

D) $x^3 + 1$

Answers and Explanations: Quick Quiz #10

1. **B**   Square everything within the parentheses, so you get $3^2 x^2 = 81$, or $9x^2 = 81$. Divide by 9 and you get $x^2 = 9$, and x could equal 3.

13. **B**   Start by trying to get a common base. This is the key to many exponent questions. Rewrite the 9 as 3^2, so the expression in question becomes $(3^2)^a 3^b$ or $3^{2a} 3^b$. Now use MADSPM rules to combine the two parts of the expression. When you multiply, you add the exponents, so the expression becomes 3^{2a+b}. Now the equation comes into play. Just substitute the value of $2a + b$ as the exponent to get 3^8.

18. **C**   Because there are variables in the answer choices, plug in. Start with an easy number, such as $x = 2$. Choice (A) is less than x, so eliminate it. Choice (B) is greater than x, so keep it. Choices (C) and (D) is greater than x, so keep them as well. Now try a different type of number. If you try 0 or a fraction, you'll get rid of (B), but not (C) or (D). Try a negative number, such as −3. While (C) is still greater than x, (D) is not.

PROBABILITY AND ARRANGEMENTS

Probability measures the likelihood something will happen:

$$\text{Probability} = \frac{\text{What You Want}}{\text{What You Have}}$$

Here's an example:

> In a small garden of flowers, 3 are daisies, 4 are sunflowers, 2 are gardenias, and 3 are carnations. If a flower is selected at random, what is the probability that it will be a gardenia?

Solution: As there are 2 gardenias, the numerator of the fraction is 2. As there are 12 flowers in all, the denominator of the fraction is 12. Thus, the probability of selecting a gardenia is $\frac{2}{12}$ or $\frac{1}{6}$.

Questions about **arrangements** ask such questions as how many ways there are to order something or how many outfits are possible. These are easy to solve if you follow the steps shown for this example:

> A restaurant offers a three-course dinner menu from which a person can select 1 of 4 appetizers, 1 of 5 main courses, and 1 of 3 desserts. How many different combinations of appetizer, main course, and dessert are possible?

As we are selecting three different items, first draw three slots as place-holders:

_____ _____ _____

Let's use the first slot for appetizers. How many appetizers are there, any one of which might be selected? 4, so write 4 above the slot. The next slot is for main course. How many main courses are there, any one of which can be selected? 5, so write 5 above the slot. The final slot is for dessert. As there are 3 desserts from which the selection can be made, write 3 in that slot. Your slots now look like this:

4   5 3

The final step is to multiply: $4 \times 5 \times 3 = 60$. That's it!

QUICK QUIZ #11

Easy

3			

	Gender		Total
Language	Boys	Girls	
French	5	11	16
Spanish	8	6	14
Total	13	17	30

The table above shows the distribution of the gender and the language studied of the 30 students in an after-school language program. If a student is chosen at random, what is the probability that the student will be either a boy studying French or a girl studying Spanish?

A) $\dfrac{3}{30}$

B) $\dfrac{10}{30}$

C) $\dfrac{11}{30}$

D) $\dfrac{13}{30}$

Medium

11			

In a drawer that contains only black, blue, and brown socks, the probability of selecting a black pair of socks is $\dfrac{3}{8}$, and there are $\dfrac{1}{3}$ as many blue pairs of socks as there are black pairs of socks. If there are 12 brown pairs of socks, how many socks are there in the drawer?

A) 16

B) 24

C) 32

D) 48

Hard

25 ▮▮▮▮▮▮▮▮▮▮▮▮▮▮▮▮▮▮▮▮▮▮▮▮

Janice has 3 belts (one blue, one red, and one green), 3 bracelets (one blue, one red, and one green), and 3 scarves (one blue, one red, and one green). If Janice wants to create an outfit containing a belt, a bracelet, and a scarf such that each item is a different color, how many possible outfits can she create?

A) 6

B) 9

C) 21

D) 27

Answers and Explanations: Quick Quiz #11

3. **C**   Remember that probability is defined as "what you want" over "what you have." Find the necessary applicable numbers from the chart. In this case, you have 30 total students, so that's the denominator. You can also tell this by looking at the answer choices. Now look for what you want: the number of boys studying French or the number of girls studying Spanish. Since you don't care if you have one or the other, you'll add these numbers. There are 5 boys studying French and 6 girls studying Spanish, so you have 11 possible candidates. Therefore, (C) is the correct answer.

11. **B**   You can Plug In the Answers. Start with (C). If $\frac{3}{8}$ of the pairs of socks are black, there are 12 pairs of black socks ($\frac{3}{8} \times 32$). As there are $\frac{1}{3}$ as many pairs of blue socks as pairs of black socks, there are 4 pairs of blue socks ($\frac{1}{3} \times 12$). Add the 12 pairs of brown socks to the pairs of black and blue socks to get 28 socks—not 32. At this point, it may not be clear whether to pick a bigger number or a smaller number, so just pick a direction. If the answer is even further off, then switch directions. Try a smaller number. If $\frac{3}{8}$ of the pairs of socks are black, there are 9 pairs of black socks ($\frac{3}{8} \times 24$). As there are $\frac{1}{3}$ as many pairs of blue socks as pairs of black socks, there are 3 pairs of blue socks ($\frac{1}{3} \times 9$). Add the 12 pairs of brown socks to the pairs of black and blue socks to get 24 socks—exactly what you wanted.

25.   **A**   Set up a slot for each of the three items. Start with the belt. How many belts are there, any one of which Janice might select? 3, so write 3 in the first slot. Move on to the bracelet. This time, there are only 2 bracelets she might choose, as she has already chosen a belt in a particular color—that color cannot be repeated. So, write 2 in the second slot. From the scarves, Janice may select only 1, as the other two colors are already chosen, so write 1 in the last slot. Multiply to get 6. If you picked (D), you did not account for the restriction on colors; there are 27 possible combinations, but only 6 involving all three colors.

SEQUENCES

Sequence questions may show up in a couple of ways on the SAT. The first way involves a repeating pattern in a set of numbers. To attack questions like this, write out the pattern until it repeats itself. Then extend the pattern until you can answer the question.

If imaginary number $i = \sqrt{-1}$, which of the following is equivalent to i^{85} ?

Start by writing out powers of i.

$$i = \sqrt{-1}$$

$$i^2 = -1$$

$$i^3 = i^2 \times i = -i$$

$$i^4 = i^2 \times i^2 = 1$$

$$i^5 = i^2 \times i^3 = i$$

$$i^6 = (i^2)^3 = -1$$

$$i^7 = i^3 \times i^4 = -i$$

$$i^8 = (i^2)^4 = 1$$

As you can see, the pattern repeats every 4 numbers, so look for a multiple of 4 that's near 85. One that's close is 84, so i^{84} equals 1, then i^{85} goes back to i again.

If all this stuff about strange patterns of i is making you nervous, don't worry. Most of the SAT sticks to real numbers and to more predictable sequences. The main two are called arithmetic and geometric sequences.

An **arithmetic sequence** is one in which each new term is obtained by adding or subtracting the same number. Examples include {1, 4, 7, 10, 13} and {10, 5, 0, –5, –10}. The question may refer to the "common difference" between terms in the sequence. In our examples, it's +3 in the first one and –5 in the second one. You may also see words like "linear increase" or "linear decrease" in the question. These refer to the fact that graphs of arithmetic sequences are straight lines in the xy-plane.

A **geometric sequence** is one in which each new term is obtained by multiplying or dividing by the same number. Examples include {1, 4, 16, 64, 256} and {100, 50, 25, 12.5, 6.25}. The question may refer to the "common ratio" between terms in the sequence. In our examples, it's 4 in the first one and $\frac{1}{2}$ in the second one. You may also see words like "exponential increase," "growth," "exponential decrease," or "decay" in the question. These refer to the fact that there is an exponent in the equation. The graphs of these in the xy-plane will be curved, not straight, lines.

There are actually some handy formulas for **growth and decay**. When the growth is a **multiple** of the total population, as we had with our geometric sequences, the formula for exponential growth or decay is

$$final\ amount = original\ amount\ (multiplier)^{number\ of\ changes}$$

Sometimes, the population changes by a constant **percent** of the total population over time, and the formula for that is

$$final\ amount = original\ amount\ (1 \pm rate)^{number\ of\ changes}$$

Knowing these formulas can help you save time and make tricky questions a bit easier.

QUICK QUIZ #12

Medium

11

The first three numbers of a sequence are 1, 3, and 5, respectively. Every number in the sequence beyond the first three numbers can be found by taking the three preceding numbers, subtracting the second from the first, and adding the third. Which of the following is the sum of the first 40 numbers of the above sequence?

A) 6

B) 12

C) 24

D) 120

12

The number of bacteria in a colony is estimated over the course of 9 days, as shown in the table below.

Time (days)	Number of Bacteria
0	50
3	500
6	5,000
9	50,000

Which of the following best describes the relationship between time and the estimated number of bacteria over these 9 days?

A) Linear decrease

B) Linear increase

C) Exponential decay

D) Exponential growth

Hard

37

The balance of a savings account at a certain bank is $280 today. The customer knows that the balance will gain 4 percent interest each year for the next 2 years. The customer uses the equation $B = 280(x)^y$ to model the balance, B, of the account after y years. To the nearest dollar, what does the customer estimate the value of the account will be at the end of two years if no money is deposited or withdrawn? (Note: Disregard the $ sign when gridding your answer.)

Answers and Explanations: Quick Quiz #12

11. **D** If you follow the sequence out, the next number is 3, and then if you keep following the instructions, the sequence repeats itself (1,3,5,3 1,3,5,3 1,3,5,3 1,3,5,3) in sets of 4. So, take the first four numbers and find the sum (12) and multiply by 10 since you actually want the first 40 numbers.

12. **D** Start with POE. The numbers are clearly increasing, so eliminate (A) and (C), which indicate a decrease. Now figure out what kind of sequence these numbers represent. Is the same number added each time? No, the numbers increase very quickly, which means this is not a linear relationship. Eliminate (B). You could calculate that the number of bacteria is multiplied by 10 every 3 days, indicating exponential growth, but (D) is the only answer left anyway.

37. **303** If you remember the parts of the growth formula, you can plug them into the function to make your calculations easier. The value in the parentheses is (1 + rate), and the rate is 4% or 0.04, so the number in parentheses is (1.04). The exponent is the number of changes, which is 2 years in this case. So the equation becomes $B = 280(1.04)^2 = 302.848$. To the nearest dollar, that's $303. If you forget the formula, you can still do this problem on your calculator. Just take it one year at a time. After the first year, the value of the original $280 will increase by 4% of 280, or by 0.04(280) = 11.2. So the total after one year is 280 + 11.2 = 291.2. For the second year, it will increase by 4% of this new total, or by 11.648. The total now will be $302.848, or $303.

Chapter 3
Algebra

In the section on strategy, we gave you some ways to avoid algebra altogether—but you still need to be able to work with simple equations and review some other algebraic principles that don't exactly crop up in everyday life.

SIMPLE EQUATIONS

Sometimes you can plug in with these, sometimes not. You will definitely need to be comfortable manipulating equations to do well on the SAT.

To solve a simple equation, get the variable on one side of the equals sign and the numbers on the other.

$$9x - 4 = 12 + x$$

$$8x - 4 = 12$$

$$8x = 16$$

$$x = 2$$

We just added 4 to both sides and subtracted x from both sides. Then we divided both sides by 8. You can add, subtract, multiply, or divide either side of an equation, but remember that what you do to one side you have to do to the other.

Polynomial equations look tricky but follow all the same rules of simple equations. You can add and subtract like terms—terms that have the same variables raised to the same powers.

What is the value of z if $3z + 4z + 7z = -42$?

In this case, the terms all have the same variable and are all to the same power. Thus, we can combine them to get $14z = -42$.

Now we'll divide each side by 14 and get $z = -3$.

Many times, however, it won't be that simple. Look at this example.

$$4x^2 - 3x + 5$$

$$2x^2 - 9x + 1$$

Which of the following is the sum of the two polynomials shown above?

A) $6x^2 + 12x + 6$

B) $6x^2 - 12x + 6$

C) $6x^4 + 12x^2 + 6$

D) $6x^4 - 12x^2 + 6$

$6x^2 - 12x + 6$

Add one pair of terms at a time. The $4x^2$ and the $2x^2$ have the same variable and base, so they can be added to get $6x^2$. The answer choices have a couple of options that start this way and a couple that start with $6x^4$. As soon as you add the first pair of terms, look to the answer choices to eliminate any that don't match. Eliminate (C) and (D). The next pair of terms, $-3x$ and $-9x$, can also be added to get $-12x$. Again eliminate answers that don't match, like (A). The complete answer is seen in (B), but you likely won't have to add all the terms together if you wisely use POE.

To solve a proportion, cross-multiply:

$$\frac{3}{x} = \frac{1}{2}$$

$$x = 6$$

Remember that you can't cancel across an equals sign!

QUICK QUIZ #1

Easy

3

If $\dfrac{3x}{5} = \dfrac{x+2}{3}$, what is the value of x?

A) $\dfrac{1}{2}$

B) 1

C) 2

D) $2\dfrac{1}{2}$

$$\left(\frac{3x}{5}\right) = \left(\frac{x+2}{3}\right)3$$

$$15x = 3x + 6$$
$$-3x$$
$$\frac{12x}{12} = \frac{6}{12}$$
$$x = 1/2$$

Medium

6

If $\dfrac{5}{x} = \dfrac{y}{10}$ and $x - y = y$, what is the value of $y + x$?

A) 5

B) 10

C) 15

D) 25

Hard

25

If 40 percent of x is equal to 160 percent of y, what is the value of $\dfrac{x}{y}$?

A) $\dfrac{1}{12}$

B) $\dfrac{1}{4}$

C) 4

D) 20

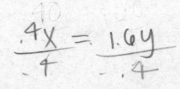

$$\frac{.4x}{.4} = \frac{1.6y}{.4}$$

$$x = .4y$$

Answers and Explanations: Quick Quiz #1

3. **D**   Cross-multiply, and you get $9x = 5(x + 2)$. Solve for x:

$$9x = 5x + 10$$

$$4x = 10$$

$$x = 2\frac{1}{2}$$

6. **C**   Plug in 10 for x and 5 for y. Both equations are satisfied by those numbers. So $y + x = 15$.

Just to show you the kind of algebra that you'd be forced to do if you didn't plug in—first, cross-multiply to get $xy = 50$. Your other equation is $x - y = y$, so $x = 2y$. Substitute that x into the first equation, and you get $2y^2 = 50$, or $y^2 = 25$. So $y = 5$. Substitute $y = 5$ into either equation and solve for x. You get $x = 10$. Now add them up and you get $x + y = 15$. A lot more work, huh? If you don't plug in when you can, it's really going to slow you down. And that's the least of it. You're also more likely to get the question wrong because the algebra takes so many steps.

25. **C**   Although you can plug in for one of the variables and solve for the other, you may find it easier to translate English into Math, and then isolate the two variables. As *percent* means "over 100," *of* means "times," and *is equal to* means "equals," the expression can be rewritten as follows:

$$\frac{40}{100} \cdot x = \frac{160}{100} \cdot y$$

Reduce the two fractions:

$$\frac{2}{5} \cdot x = \frac{8}{5} \cdot y$$

Now, isolate the variables on one side of the equation and the numbers on the other side. So, divide both sides by y, and multiply both sides by $\frac{5}{2}$:

$$\frac{x}{y} = \frac{8}{5} \times \frac{5}{2} = \frac{8}{2} = 4$$

QUADRATIC EQUATIONS

Even the name is scary. What does it mean, anyway? No matter. All you need to know are a few simple things: factoring and recognizing perfect squares.

To factor, first draw a pair of empty parentheses. Deal with the first term, then the signs, then the last term. For example:

$$x^2 + x - 12 \qquad (\quad)(\quad)$$
$$(x \quad)(x \quad) \dots \text{first term}$$
$$(x + \quad)(x - \quad) \dots \text{signs}$$
$$(x + 4)(x - 3) \dots \text{last term}$$

Check your factoring by multiplying the terms:

first term = $x \bullet x = x^2$

inner term = $4x$

outer term = $-3x$

last term = $4 \times -3 = -12$

Then add them up:

$$x^2 + 4x + -3x + -12 = x^2 + x - 12$$

Some guidelines:

If the last term is positive, your signs will be either +, + or −, −.

If the last term is negative, your signs will be +, −.

Your first try may not be right—don't be afraid to mess around with it a little.

To recognize the difference of two squares, memorize the following:

$$(x + y)(x - y) = x^2 - y^2$$

This format works whether you have variables, as above, or numbers:

$$57^2 - 43^2 = (57 + 43)(57 - 43) = 100 \times 14 = 1,400$$

One more thing—memorize the following:

$$(x + y)^2 = (x + y)(x + y) = x^2 + 2xy + y^2$$
$$(x - y)^2 = (x - y)(x - y) = x^2 - 2xy + y^2$$

> When you see anything that looks like one form of these expressions, try converting to its other form. That should lead you straight to the correct answer.

QUICK QUIZ #2

Easy

7

If $\dfrac{x^2 + 5x + 6}{x + 2} = 12$, what is the value of x?

A) −2
B) 2
C) 3
(D) 9

$$\frac{(x+3)(x+2)}{(x+2)}$$

$$x+3 = 12$$
$$-3 \qquad -3$$
$$x = 9$$

Medium

15

If $a - b = 3$ and $a^2 - b^2 = 21$, what is the value of a?

A) −3
B) −2
C) 2
D) 5

Hard

29

If $x < 0$ and $(2x - 1)^2 = 25$, what is the value of x^2?

A) −2
B) 3
C) 4
D) 9

7. **D** First, factor the expression to $(x + 3)(x + 2)$. Now you have $\frac{(x+3)(x+2)}{x+2} = 12$. The $(x + 2)$ cancels, and you have $x + 3 = 12$, so $x = 9$. Or you could Plug In the Answers: If $x = 9$, $\frac{9^2 + 5(9) + 6}{9 + 2} = 12$, or $\frac{132}{11} = 12$. It looks funny, but it works.

15. **D** Factor $a^2 - b^2$ to equal $(a + b)(a - b) = 21$. If $a - b = 3$, then $a + b = 7$. Here you could do one of two things. You can try some different numbers and see what satisfies both simple equations, or you could add the two equations together and get $2a = 10$ and $a = 5$.

29. **C** Lots of algebra:

$$(2x - 1)^2 = 25$$

$$(2x - 1)(2x - 1) = 25$$

$$4x^2 - 4x + 1 = 25$$

$$4x^2 - 4x - 24 = 0$$

$$x^2 - x - 6 = 0$$

$$(x - 3)(x + 2) = 0$$

So x can be 3 or –2. If x is negative, it has to be –2, and $-2^2 = 4$. You could also Plug In, but you have to remember that the question asks for x^2, not x. That means (C) and (D) are good answers to try, since they're squares.

Don't forget that one of your main jobs on the SAT is following directions. If you picked (A) or (B), we suspect you did most of the problem correctly but forgot that x is negative, or failed to square x. Don't let carelessness rob you of your hard-earned points!

SIMULTANEOUS EQUATIONS

Two different equations, two different variables. You will not usually have to solve for both variables.

To solve simultaneous equations, stack 'em up, and either add or subtract:

If $2x + 3y = 12$ and $3x - 3y = -2$, what is the value of x ?

$$
\begin{array}{r}
2x + 3y = 12 \\
+\ 3x - 3y = -2 \\
\hline
5x = 10 \\
x = 2
\end{array}
$$

If we had subtracted, we'd have gotten $-x + 6y = 14$, which wouldn't get us anywhere. If you choose the wrong operation, no big deal, just try the other one.

> Don't automatically start solving for x and y—you may not need to.
> Focus on what the question is specifically asking.

Sometimes, you won't have to solve for either of the variables. One situation involves slopes of lines, which we'll cover in the next chapter. In another situation, you'll have to determine the equations that could be used to solve for the variables in the context of a long word problem. These aren't too bad if you translate one piece of information at a time and use Process of Elimination.

8

A ferry is used to transport vehicles that weigh either 2 tons or 2.5 tons each. Let a be the number of 2-ton vehicles and b be the number of 2.5-ton vehicles. The ferry can transport up to either 34 vehicles or a weight of 74 tons. Which of the following systems of inequalities represents this relationship?

A) $\begin{cases} \dfrac{a}{2} + \dfrac{b}{2.5} \le 74 \\ a + b \le 34 \end{cases}$

B) $\begin{cases} a + b \le 74 \\ 2a + 2.5b \le 74 \end{cases}$

C) $\begin{cases} 2a + 2.5b \le 34 \\ a + b \le 74 \end{cases}$

D) $\begin{cases} 2a + 2.5b \le 74 \\ a + b \le 34 \end{cases}$

Solution: First, translate the one piece of information that seems most straightforward. You may decide that the upper limit on the total number of vehicles, 34, is the best place to start. The total number of vehicles includes both 2-ton vehicles (a) and 2.5-ton vehicles (b), so $a + b \leq 34$. Now eliminate any answer choices that do not include this inequality: (B) and (C). The difference between the remaining answers is what is less than or equal to 74. That number refers to the total weight the ferry can hold, which will again be made up of 2-ton and 2.5-ton vehicles. To get the total weight, you'd multiply the weight of each vehicle category by the number of vehicles in that category and then add up all the category weights. For 2-ton vehicles, it would be 2 times the number of 2-ton vehicles, (a), so the correct answer must have $2a$ in it. Add in the weight of the 2.5-ton vehicles, $2.5b$, and you get (D) as the correct answer.

QUICK QUIZ #3

Easy

5

If $3x + 5y = 15$ and $x - 2y = 10$, what is the value of $2x + 7y$?

A) 5

B) 10

C) 15

D) 25

Medium

7

$$3c - 4d = -11$$
$$4c - 3d = -3$$

If (c, d) is a solution to the system of equations above, what is the value of $c - d$?

A)   8

B) −2

C) −8

D) −14

Hard

33

At a conference, 94 salespeople are discussing effective strategies to expand a customer base. The discussion has been divided into 20 subtopics, and each subtopic will be discussed by a group of either 4 or 6 salespeople. How many of the subtopics will be discussed by a group of 6 salespeople?

Answers and Explanations: Quick Quiz #3

5. **A**   Stack 'em and subtract:

$$\begin{array}{ll} 3x+5y=15 & \quad 3x+5y=15 \\ -(x-2y=10) & \quad \underline{-x-2y=-10} \\ & \quad 2x+7y=5 \end{array}$$

That's it. You don't have to solve for x or y individually. Less work is good. (Be careful with the signs when you subtract one equation from another.)

7. **B**   Start with the easiest option: Add the equations together to see if you get what you want.

$$3c - 4d = -11$$

$$\underline{+\ 4c - 3d = -3}$$

$$7c - 7d = -14$$

That's not exactly $c - d$, but if you divide the whole equation by 7, you'll get $c - d$ on the left and -2 on the right. So the answer is (B).

33. **7**   This one will take some translation before you can solve anything. Let's call the groups with four people f and those with 6 people s. There are going to be 20 groups altogether, so $f + s = 20$. The number of people in 4-person groups can be found by multiplying 4 by f, and the number of people in 6-person groups is $6s$. Add those together to get the total number of people, which is 94. So the second equation is $4f + 6s = 94$. With two equations and two variables, you can solve for s, which is the value the question asks for. Start by stacking and adding the equations.

$$4f + 6s = 94$$

$$f + s = 20$$

As you can see, just adding or subtracting them won't isolate s, and solving and substituting could take a while. You need to manipulate the equations so that when you add them together, the f's disappear. To do this, multiply the second equation by -4 to get $-4f - 4s = -80$. Now stack and add.

$$4f + 6s = 94$$

$$\underline{-4f - 4s = -80}$$

$$2s = 14$$

Divide both sides by 2 to find that $s = 7$, and you're done!

INEQUALITIES

Treat these just like equations, but remember one rule: **If you multiply or divide by a negative number, the sign changes direction.**

$$x + 6 > 10 \qquad\qquad 2x > 16 \qquad\qquad -2x > 16$$

$$x > 4 \qquad\qquad\qquad x > 8 \qquad\qquad\quad x < -8$$

> It's very easy to mix up the direction of the > or < sign. Be extra careful.

QUICK QUIZ #4

Easy

3

If $3x + 7 < 5x - 4$, which of the following is true?

A) $\dfrac{11}{2} < x$

B) $x < \dfrac{3}{2}$

C) $x < \dfrac{11}{8}$

D) $\dfrac{11}{2} > x$

Handwritten work:
$$3x + 7 < 5x - 4$$
$$3x \qquad\qquad -3x$$
$$7 < 2x - 4$$
$$+4 \qquad\qquad +4$$
$$\frac{11}{2} < \frac{2x}{2} \qquad \frac{11}{2} < x$$

Medium

11

If $3b + 8 > 6 + 2b$, and b is a negative integer, what is the value of b?

A) 0

B) −1

C) −2

D) −3

Handwritten work:
$$3b + 8 > 6 + 2b$$
$$3(-1) + 8 > 6 + 2(-1) \qquad 3(-2) + 8 > 6 + 2(-1)$$
$$-3 + 8 \qquad\qquad\qquad -6 + 8$$
$$5 > 4 \qquad\qquad\qquad\qquad 2 > 4$$

Hard

22

A mail clerk estimates that a package will cost f dollars to ship, where $f > 20$. His goal is for the estimate to be within 2 dollars of the actual cost to ship the package. If the mail clerk meets his goal and it costs g dollars to ship the package, which of the following inequalities represents the relationship between the estimated cost and the actual shipping cost?

A) $-2 < g - f < 2$

B) $g > f + 2$

C) $g < f - 2$

D) $f + g < 2$

Answers and Explanations: Quick Quiz #4

3.   **A**   Treat the inequality just like an equation—subtract $3x$ from both sides, and you get $7 < 2x - 4$. Add 4 to both sides to get $11 < 2x$. Divide through by 2, which leaves you with $\frac{11}{2} < x$.

11. **B**   Move the bs to one side and the integers to the other, and you get $b > -2$. If b is a negative integer, the only possibility is -1.

22. **A**   The question already states that $f > 20$, so (D) wouldn't make sense. Eliminate (D). Now use Plugging In to see what would happen. Say $f = 25$. One value of g that works is 26, since it is within 2 dollars of 25. Choice (A) becomes $-2 < 26 - 25 < 2$. This is true, so keep it. Choice (B) becomes $26 > 25 + 2$, which is not true and can be eliminated. Choice (C) becomes $26 < 25 - 2$, which is also false, so (A) is the correct answer.

FUNCTIONS

Functions will be tested in many ways on the SAT, and the test will use the standard mathematic notation $f(x)$ for a function named f.

If $f(x) = 2x^2 + 4x + 12$, what is the value of $f(4)$?

Don't be distracted by the fancy symbols; just pop the number into the function and crank out the answer. We want the $f(4)$, so wherever there is an x in the function, we'll replace it with a 4.

$$f(4) = 2(4)^2 + 4(4) + 12$$
$$= 2(16) + 16 + 12$$
$$= 60$$

Of course, the SAT will deal with concepts beyond testing which values of $f(x)$ will result from putting in a certain value of x or which values of x will yield a specific result for $f(x)$ or y. One advanced concept is related to the factors of a function, which can give you the roots or zeroes of that function.

8

x	$g(x)$
-1	6
0	4
3	1
5	0

The function g is defined by a polynomial. Some of the values of x and $g(x)$ are shown in the table above. Which of the following must be a factor of g ?

A) $x - 6$

B) $x - 5$

C) $x - 4$

D) $x - 3$

Solution: When you factor a polynomial, you can set each factor equal to zero to find the roots. These are the places where the function crosses the x-axis, or the x-values for which $f(x)$ or y equal zero. In this question, you can work backwards from y or $g(x) = 0$. This happens when $x = 5$. For the factor to equal zero, you solve for zero by subtracting 5 from both sides to get $x - 5 = 0$. Therefore, $x - 5$ is a factor of the polynomial, and (B) is the answer.

QUICK QUIZ #5

Easy

4

If $f(x) = 2x^2 + 3$, for which of the following values of x does $f(x) = 21$?

A) −9

B) −3

C) 0

D) 1

Medium

9

$$h(x) = cx^2 + 18$$

For the function h defined above, c is a constant and $h(2) = 10$. What is the value of $h(-2)$?

A) −10

B) −2

C) 10

D) 18

Hard

23

The height of the steam burst of a certain geyser varies with the length of time since the previous steam burst. The longer the time since the last burst, the greater the height of the steam burst. If t is the time in hours since the previous steam burst and H is the height in meters of the steam burst, which of the following could express the relationship of t and H ?

A) $H(t) = \dfrac{1}{2}(t - 7)$

B) $H(t) = \dfrac{2}{t - 7}$

C) $H(t) = 2 - (t - 7)$

D) $H(t) = 7 - 2t$

Answers and Explanations: Quick Quiz #5

4. **B**   In this case, Plug in the Answers for the value of x, starting with (C). Plugging in 0 for x gives you $f(0) = 2(0)^2 + 3 = 3$. But you want $f(x) = 21$, so eliminate (C). Now try (B): $f(-3) = 21$, so this is the right answer. Alternatively, set $f(x) = 21$, and solve $21 = 2x^2 + 3$.

9. **C**   If you are a Zen master of algebra, you may recognize that this function is a parabola. Parabolas are symmetrical about a center line, and since there is no number added or subtracted in parentheses [such as $(x - 2)^2$], this parabola is symmetrical about the y-axis. As such, any value of x will give the same y-value as $-x$ will, so $h(2) = h(-2) = 10$.

    If you are thinking, "Wait, what?" right now—never fear! Your old friend Plugging In can come to the rescue here. Plug $x = 2$ into the function to get $h(2) = c(2)^2 + 18 = 4c + 18$. The question says this is 10, so you have $4c + 18 = 10$. Subtract 18 from both sides to get $4c = -8$, so $c = -2$. Now you have the full function, $-2x^2 + 18$, and can easily Plug In (-2). You get $h(-2) = -2(-2)^2 + 18 = -2(4) + 18 = -8 + 18 = 10$. Either way, the answer is (C).

23. **A**   The relationship is the greater the time, the greater the height. So the correct function is one that yields a greater H as you increase t. Try plugging in for t in the functions to see which one increases as t increases. Try $t = 10$ and $t = 20$. Only (A) has a greater H for $t = 20$ than it does for $t = 10$. That is $\frac{1}{2}(10 - 7) < \frac{1}{2}(20 - 7)$. The answer is (A).

Chapter 4
Additional Topics

This chapter will cover some topics that may not be tested as often. Tackle these once you've mastered the strategies and content in the previous chapters.

GEOMETRY

You're not going to believe how simple this is. Just a few rules, a couple of formulas, and your common sense. And don't forget about estimating.

Definitions

arc	part of a circumference
area	the space inside a two-dimensional figure
bisect	cut in two equal parts
chord	a line that goes through a circle, but does not go through the center; it will always be shorter than the diameter
circumference	the distance around a circle
diagonal	a line from one corner of a square to its opposite corner
diameter	a line directly through the center of a circle; the longest line you can draw in a circle
equidistant	exactly in the middle
equilateral	a triangle with three equal sides, therefore three equal angles (60° each)
hypotenuse	the longest leg of a right triangle, opposite the right angle
isosceles	a triangle with two equal sides and two equal angles
parallel	lines that will never intersect (think railroad tracks)
perimeter	the distance around a figure
perpendicular	two lines that intersect to form 90-degree angles
quadrilateral	any four-sided figure
radius	a line from the center of a circle to the edge of the circle (half the diameter)
volume	the space inside a three-dimensional figure

LINES AND ANGLES

A line has 180°, so the angles formed by any cut to your line will add up to 180°:

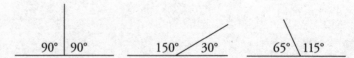

Two intersecting lines form a pair of **vertical angles,** which are equal:

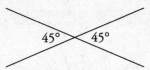

Parallel lines cut by a third line will form two kinds of angles: big ones and little ones. All the big ones are equal to each other; all the little ones are equal to each other. Any big angle plus any little angle will equal 180°:

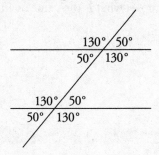

QUICK QUIZ #1

Easy

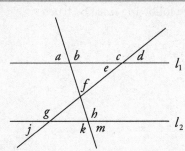

In the figure above, l_1 is parallel to l_2. Which of the following angles are NOT equal?

A) c and g

B) b and h

C) a and m

D) a and k

Medium

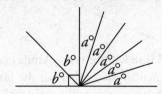

10

In the figure above, what is the value of $4a - b$?

A) $18°$

B) $27°$

C) $45°$

D) $54°$

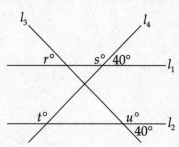

Note: Figure not drawn to scale.

Which of the following must be true?

A) $l_1 \parallel l_2$

B) l_3 bisects l_4

C) $s = t$

D) $u = 140°$

Answers and Explanations: Quick Quiz #1

4. **D** Start with (A) and cross off as you go along. In (D), $a = m$, not k. Keep in mind that the two lines cutting through l_1 and l_2 aren't parallel, and so the angles made by one line have no relationship to the angles made by the other line.

10. **B** Estimate first. Outline the measurement of four of the a's. That's about 60. Now pretend you are subtracting b, about 45. How much is left? Not so much, right? Cross out (D). Now do the math: $2b = 90°$, so $b = 45°$. $5a = 90$, so $a = 18°$. Now plug those numbers into the equation: $4(18) - 45 = 27$.

18.   **D**   This question is actually very easy, as long as you don't pick the first answer that looks halfway decent before reading (D). Angle *u* has to be 140° because it's on a straight line with the angle marked 40°. All the other answers look like they're true, but you can't know for certain. The only thing you know for sure is that angles on the same line add up to 180°, and vertical angles are equal. None of these lines are necessarily parallel, so you can't assume anything else.

TRIANGLES

Triangles have 180°.

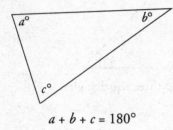

$$a + b + c = 180°$$

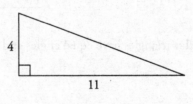

$$50° + 20° + 110° = 180°$$

Area = $\frac{1}{2} bh$

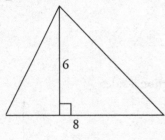

$$\text{area} = \frac{1}{2}(8)(6) = 24$$

$$\text{area} = \frac{1}{2}(11)(4) = 22$$

Perimeter: Add up the sides.

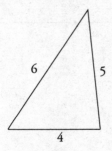

Perimeter = 15

Right triangles have a right, or 90°, angle:

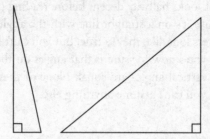

Isosceles triangles have two equal sides and two equal angles:

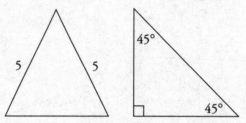

Equilateral triangles have three equal sides and three equal angles:

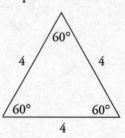

Similar triangles have equal angles and proportional sides:

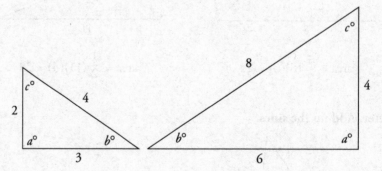

The Wonderful World of Right Triangles

For any right triangle, if you know the lengths of two of the sides, you can figure out the length of the third side by using the Pythagorean Theorem:

$$a^2 + b^2 = c^2$$

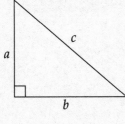

$$a^2 + b^2 = c^2$$

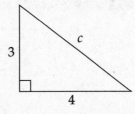

$$3^2 + 4^2 = c^2$$
$$25 = c^2$$
$$5 = c$$

However, you often don't even need to use the theorem, because the test-writers sometimes create right triangles that feature these common Pythagorean triples.

3:4:5   6:8:10   5:12:13

In two special cases, you only have to know one side to figure out the other two, because the sides are in a constant ratio.

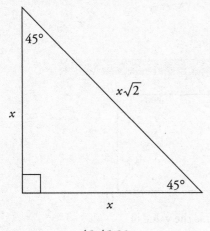

45:45:90

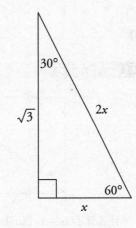

30:60:90

QUICK QUIZ #2

Easy

5

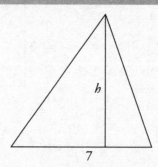

In the triangle above, *h* is perpendicular to the base and the area equals 21. What is the value of *h* ?

A) 3

B) 4

C) 6

D) 7

Medium

14

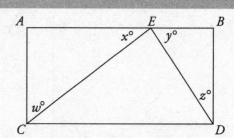

If *ABCD* is a rectangle, what is the value of $w + x + y + z$?

A)   90

B)   150

C)   180

D)   210

Hard

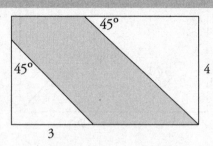

Note: Figure not drawn to scale.

If the rectangle above has an area of 32, and the unshaded triangles are isosceles, what is the perimeter of the shaded area?

A) 16

B) $10 + 7\sqrt{2}$

C) $10 + 12\sqrt{2}$

D) 32

Answers and Explanations: Quick Quiz #2

5. **C**   Estimate first—it's drawn to scale. If the base is 7, how long does the height look? About the same? Cross out at least (A), as well as (B) if you're feeling confident. Now do the math: area = $\frac{1}{2}$ bh, so $\frac{1}{2}$ (7h) = 21, and h = 6. It would be easy to pick (A) if you weren't paying attention, because $7 \times 3 = 21$, and so it seems appealing.

14. **C**   If you picked (A) or (D), you didn't estimate. See how the rectangle is cut up into three triangles? Each of those triangles has 180°. Both of the triangles with marked angles also have right angles because they're corners of a rectangle. So $\triangle ACE + \triangle EBD = 360°$. Subtract the two right angles, and you're left with 180°.

20. **B**   First, write in everything you know: If the area is 32, the length is 8. That means the base is 3 + 5 and the left side is 1 + 3. The triangles in opposing corners are both 45-45-90 triangles: The one on the base has a hypotenuse of $3\sqrt{2}$, and the one with sides of 4 has a hypotenuse of $4\sqrt{2}$. Add up all the sides of the shaded part, and you get $10 + 7\sqrt{2}$.

Here's how it should look:

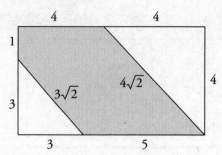

CIRCLES

Circles have 360°. Area = πr^2.

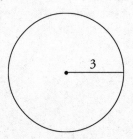

$$\text{Circumference} = 2\pi r$$
$$r = 3$$
$$C = 2\pi(3) = 6\pi$$
$$A = \pi(3)^2 = 9\pi$$

For any pie slice of a circle, the central angle, arc, and area are in proportion to the whole circle.

$$\frac{\text{part}}{\text{whole}} = \frac{\text{central angle}}{360°} = \frac{\text{arc length}}{2\pi r} = \frac{\text{sector area}}{\pi r^2}$$

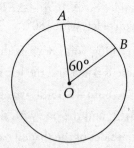

$\dfrac{60°}{360°} = \dfrac{1}{6}$, so arc AB is $\dfrac{1}{6}$ of the circumference, and pie slice AOB is $\dfrac{1}{6}$ of the total area.

QUICK QUIZ #3

Easy

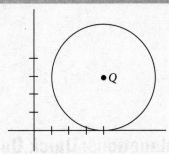

Center *Q* of the circle above has coordinates of (4, 3).
What is the circumference of the circle?

A) π

B) 2π

C) 6π

D) 9π

Medium

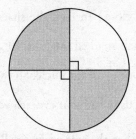

If the circumference of the circle above is 16π, what is
the total area of the shaded regions?

A) 64π

B) 32π

C) 12π

D) 8π

Hard

One circle has a radius of r, and another circle has a radius of $2r$. The area of the larger circle is how many times the area of the smaller circle?

A) 1.5

B) 2

C) 3

D) 4

Answers and Explanations: Quick Quiz #3

4. **C**   The easiest way to solve this is simply to count the number of units in the radius, which is 3. Make sure you draw a radius on the diagram—if you draw it perpendicular to the y-axis, you'll be able to count the units with no problem. If you picked (D), you found the area. Read the question carefully and give 'em what they ask for.

13. **B**   The circumference is 16π, so use the circumference formula to get the radius: $2\pi r = 16\pi$, and $r = 8$. The area of the whole circle is $\pi r^2 = \pi(8)^2 = 64\pi$. Hold on—don't pick (A). At this point, you could happily estimate the shaded area as half the circle and pick (B). (Nothing else is close.) In fact, the shaded area is exactly half of the circle because each marked angle is 90°, which makes each of those pie slices $\dfrac{90°}{360°}$, or $\dfrac{1}{4}$ of the circle. So two of them make up $\dfrac{1}{2}$ of the circle, or 32π. Trust what your eyes tell you.

20. **D**   Plug In. If $r = 2$, then the area of the small circle is 4π. The radius of the second circle is $2(2)$, or 4, so the area is 16π. The larger circle is 4 times as big as the smaller circle. (Don't you just love to plug in?)

> Notice how the hard question doesn't give you a picture or any real numbers to use. So draw the picture and make up your own numbers. Try to visualize the problem. Plugging In works just as well on geometry problems as it does on algebra problems.

Note: A very common careless error on circle problems is getting the area and circumference mixed up. Don't worry! The formulas are printed on the first page of each math section in case you forgot them.

CIRCLE EQUATIONS

You may also need to know the equation of a circle, which will tell you the center of the circle (h, k) and the radius r.

$$(x - h)^2 + (y - k)^2 = r^2$$

Use it when working with circles in the xy-plane to eliminate those with the wrong radius or center.

VOLUME

The most common shapes you'll have to find the volume of on the SAT are rectangular solids (boxes), cubes (square boxes), and possibly cylinders (cans).

For these shapes, the volume equals the area of one face × the third dimension (the depth or the height). Here are the formulas you need to know:

Rectangular Box

Volume = $l \times w \times h$

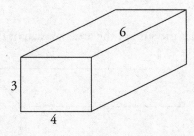

$V = lwh$
$V = 6(3)(4)$
$V = 72$

Cube

Volume = s^3

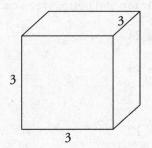

$V = s^3$
$V = 3^3$
$V = 27$

Think Inside the Box
The formulas for the volume of rectangular solids, cylinders, spheres, cones, and even pyramids will be provided in the box at the start of the math sections.

Cylinder

Volume = $\pi r^2 h$

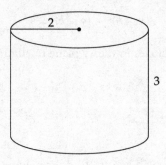

$V = \pi r^2 h$

$V = \pi 2^2(3)$

$V = 12\pi$

SURFACE AREA

The surface area of a box is the sum of the areas of each of the faces.

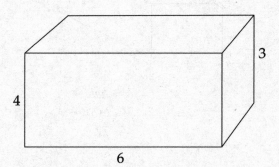

In the figure above, the front and back faces each measure 6 by 4; the side faces each measure 4 by 3; and the top and bottom faces each measure 6 by 3.

Front face (6×4) = 24

Back face (6×4) = 24

Left face (4×3) = 12

Right face (4×3) = 12

Top face (6×3) = 18

Bottom face (6×3) = 18

The surface area is the sum of these faces: 24 + 24 + 12 + 12 + 18 + 18 = 108.

QUICK QUIZ #4

Easy

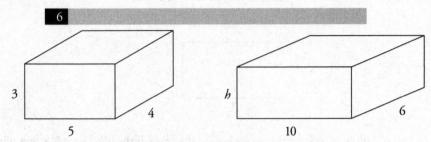

Note: Figures not drawn to scale.

If the volumes of the two boxes above are equal, what is the value of h?

A) 1

B) 2

C) 4

D) 5

Medium

9

Sam is packing toy blocks into a crate. If each block is a cube with a side of 6 inches, and the crate is 1 foot high, 2 feet long, and 2 feet wide, how many blocks can Sam fit into the crate?

A) 6

B) 12

C) 24

D) 32

Hard

19

The surface area of a rectangular solid measuring $5 \times 6 \times 8$ is how much greater than the surface area of a rectangular solid measuring $3 \times 6 \times 8$?

A) 12

B) 24

C) 48

D) 56

Answers and Explanations: Quick Quiz #4

6. **A** The box on the left has volume = $3 \times 4 \times 5 = 60$. The box on the right is then $10 \times 6 \times h = 60$. So $h = 1$. Don't forget to estimate!

9. **D** First, draw the crate. It should look like this:

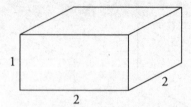

Now visualize putting blocks into the crate. If the blocks are 6 inches high, you'll be able to stack 2 rows in the crate since the crate is a foot high. Now mark off 6-inch intervals along the side of the crate. (You're dividing 2 feet, or 24 inches, by 6 inches.) You can fit 4 blocks along each side. Now multiply everything together and you get $2 \times 4 \times 4 = 32$ blocks.

You can also divide the volume of the crate by the volume of each block, as long as your units are consistent:

$$\frac{1 \text{ ft} \times 2 \text{ ft} \times 2 \text{ ft}}{\frac{1}{2}\text{ft} \times \frac{1}{2}\text{ft} \times \frac{1}{2}\text{ft}} \text{ or } \frac{12 \text{ in} \times 24 \text{ in} \times 24 \text{ in}}{6 \text{ in} \times 6 \text{ in} \times 6 \text{ in}}$$

19. **D** Find the surface area of the first figure. It has two sides 5×6, two sides 6×8, and two sides 5×8. Therefore, its surface area is $30 + 30 + 48 + 48 + 40 + 40$, which makes 236. The second figure has two sides 3×6, two sides 6×8, and two sides 3×8. Its surface area is $18 + 18 + 48 + 48 + 24 + 24$, or 180. The difference between these two surface areas is 56.

TRIGONOMETRY

The SAT may include trig questions. Understanding the basic definitions of sine, cosine, and tangent will help you answer these questions.

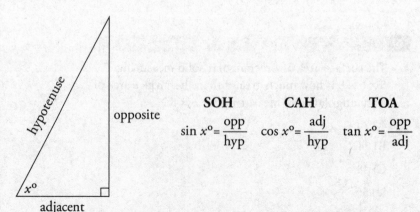

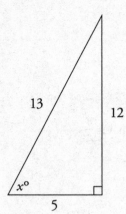

$$\sin x° = \frac{12}{13} \quad \cos x° = \frac{5}{13} \quad \tan x° = \frac{12}{5}$$

Radians and Degrees

Radians and degrees are just different units used to measure angles. Your calculator has both modes, so make sure you are using the correct mode when answering these questions.

Here is how to convert between degrees and radians (or vice versa):

$$\frac{\pi}{180} = \frac{\text{degrees}}{\text{radians}}$$

COMPLEX NUMBERS

Occasionally, a mathematical operation will require taking a square root of a negative number. With real numbers, that isn't possible—no real number can be squared to get a negative number. This is where i comes in. The i stands for "imaginary," to distinguish it from "real" numbers, and it equals $\sqrt{-1}$. When i is squared, the result is -1.

$$i = \sqrt{-1}$$
$$i^2 = -1$$
$$i^3 = -i$$
$$i^4 = 1$$

"Complex numbers" combine real and imaginary numbers in the form $a + bi$, where a is real and bi is imaginary.

QUICK QUIZ #5

Easy

8

What is the measure in degrees of an angle that is $\frac{\pi}{4}$ radians?

A) 4°

B) 25°

C) 45°

D) 90°

Medium

14

A 25-foot ladder is placed against the side of a building at an angle of 70° from the ground. How far away is the base of the ladder from the building?

A) 25 cos 70°

B) 8.5 sin 70°

C) 25 tan 70°

D) 8.5 cos 70°

Hard

15

Which of the following is equivalent to the expression $\left(\frac{6 + 3i}{2} - \frac{7 + 4i}{3}\right)^2$?

A) $\dfrac{13 + 7i}{6}$

B) $\dfrac{14 + 8i}{6}$

C) $\dfrac{4 - i}{36}$

D) $\dfrac{15 + 8i}{36}$

Answers and Explanations: Quick Quiz #5

8. **C** Use the conversion $\dfrac{\pi}{180} = \dfrac{\text{radians}}{\text{degrees}}$.

$$\frac{\pi}{180} = \frac{\frac{\pi}{4}}{x}$$

Cross-multiply:

$$180 \cdot \frac{\pi}{4} = \pi \cdot x$$
$$45 \cdot \pi = \pi \cdot x$$
$$x = 45°$$

14. **A** Remember SOHCAHTOA and draw a picture.

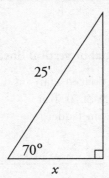

You will need to use cosine to find the answer, so eliminate (B) and (C).

$$\cos 70° = \frac{x}{25'}$$

$$x = 25 \cos 70°$$

15. **D** Find a common denominator with which to subtract the fractions by multiplying the top and bottom of the first fraction by 3 and the top and bottom of the second fraction by 2.

$$\left(\frac{18 + 9i}{6} - \frac{14 + 8i}{6} \right)^2$$

Combine.

$$\left(\frac{18 + 9i - 14 - 8i}{6} \right)^2 = \left(\frac{4 + i}{6} \right)^2 =$$

$$\frac{16 + 4i + 4i + i^2}{36} = \frac{16 + 8i + i^2}{36}$$

Remember that $i^2 = -1$, so the expression becomes $\dfrac{15 + 8i}{36}$.

COORDINATE GEOMETRY

Remember how to plot points? The first number is *x* and the second is *y*.

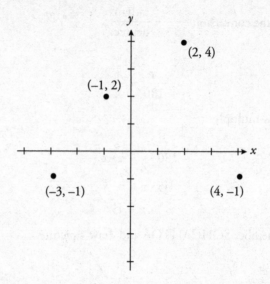

To find the length of a horizontal or vertical line, count the units:

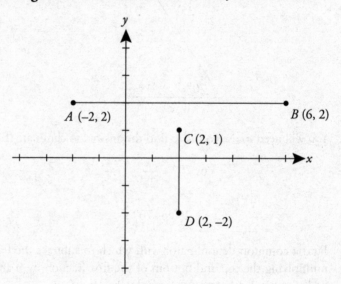

AB = 8 and *CD* = 3

To find the length of any other line, draw in a right triangle and use the Pythagorean Theorem:

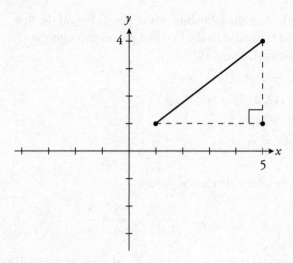

The triangle has legs of 3 and 4, so $3^2 + 4^2 = c^2$, and $c = 5$. (It's a Pythagorean triple again.)

To find the slope, put the rise over the run. The formula is

$$\textbf{slope} = \frac{y_1 - y_2}{x_1 - x_2}$$

It doesn't matter which point you begin with, just be consistent.

What is the slope of the line containing points $(2, -3)$ and $(4, 3)$?

$$\text{slope} = \frac{-3 - 3}{2 - 4} = \frac{-6}{-2} = 3 \text{ or } \frac{3 - (-3)}{4 - 2} = \frac{6}{2} = 3$$

A slope that goes from low to high is positive.

A slope that goes from high to low is negative.

A slope that goes straight across is 0.

positive slope   negative slope   0 slope

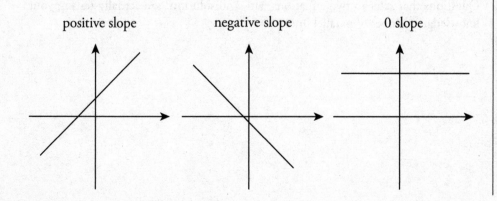

Parallel lines have equal slopes. **Perpendicular lines** have slopes that are negative reciprocals of each other. For example:

> Which of the following sets of points lies on the line
> that is parallel to the line that passes through the
> points (1, 3) and (5, 8) ?
>
> A) (−5, −8), (1, 3)
>
> B) (12, 2), (8, −3)
>
> C) (5, 3), (1,8)
>
> D) (15, 3), (6, 2)

First, find the slope of the first set of points.

$$\text{slope} = \frac{3-8}{1-5} = \frac{-5}{-4} = \frac{5}{4}$$

Then, check the answer choices and look for the set of points that has an equal slope. The correct answer is (B).

Try the same thing with perpendicular lines.

> Which of the following sets of points lies on the line
> that is perpendicular to the line that passes through
> the points (1, 3) and (5, 8) ?
>
> A) (16, 7), (11, 11)
>
> B) (8, 5), (3, 1)
>
> C) (2, 5), (3, 13)
>
> D) (7, 8), (5, 11)

We already found the slope. Now we need its negative reciprocal, which is $-\frac{4}{5}$. Check the answers. Choice (A) gives us:

$$\text{slope} = \frac{7-11}{16-11} = -\frac{4}{5}$$

Bingo!

Sometimes, a question will be about parallel lines, even if it doesn't seem like it. Questions that refer to two equations with "no solution" are actually testing your knowledge of slopes of parallel lines.

$$cx - 5y = 6$$
$$2x - 3y = 8$$

In the system of equations above, c is a constant and x and y are variables. For what value of c will the system have no solution?

A) $-\dfrac{10}{3}$

B) $-\dfrac{13}{11}$

C) $\dfrac{13}{11}$

D) $\dfrac{10}{3}$

Solution: The two equations represent two lines. If these lines have no solution, that means they never intersect and are parallel. Parallel lines have the same slope, so you need to figure out what value of c will make that happen. Start by finding the slope of the second line. In the form $Ax + By = C$, the slope is $-\dfrac{A}{B}$, or you could get it into $y = mx + b$ form, where m is the slope. Either way, the slope is $\dfrac{-2}{-3} = \dfrac{2}{3}$. For the first line, the slope is $\dfrac{-c}{-5} = \dfrac{c}{5}$. Now set the two slopes equal and cross-multiply.

$$\frac{2}{3} = \frac{c}{5}$$
$$3c = 10$$
$$c = \frac{10}{3}$$

Finally, if the question asks about two lines with "infinitely many solutions," the equations actually represent the same exact line. Of course, the equations will also have the same slope in that situation.

QUICK QUIZ #6

Easy

4

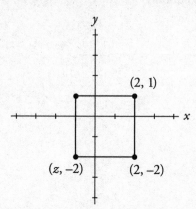

If the figure above is a square, what is the value of z ?

A) −2

B) −1

C) 1

D) 2

Medium

14

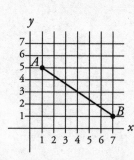

In the figure above, what is the length of AB ?

A) 4

B) $2\sqrt{6}$

C) 7

D) $\sqrt{52}$

Hard

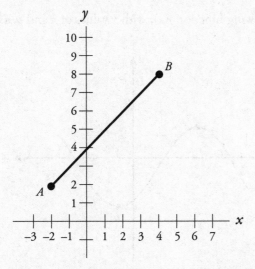

In the figure above, the coordinates for point A are $(-2, 2)$ and the coordinates for point B are $(4, 8)$. If line CD, not shown, is parallel to the line AB, what is the slope of line CD ?

A) -1

B) 0

C) 1

D) 2

Answers and Explanations: Quick Quiz #6

4. **B** Just count the units. Remember that coordinates in the lower left quadrant will always be negative.

14. **D** Use the units to measure each leg. You should get one leg = 4 and the other = 6. Now use the Pythagorean Theorem: $4^2 + 6^2 = c^2$.

$$16 + 36 = c^2$$
$$52 = c^2$$
$$\sqrt{52} = c$$

24. **C** Write in the coordinates of A and B. $A = (-2, 2)$ and $B = (4, 8)$. So the slope of $AB = \dfrac{2 - 8}{-2 - 4} = \dfrac{-6}{-6} = 1$. If CD is parallel to AB, it has the same slope. (You could draw in a parallel line and recalculate the slope, but you'd be doing extra work.)

GRAPHS OF FUNCTIONS

For graphs involving functions, you will sometimes be asked to provide info on a portion of a function or how one function was translated into another function.

Consider the following function $f(x)$, with x values of a and b, as indicated:

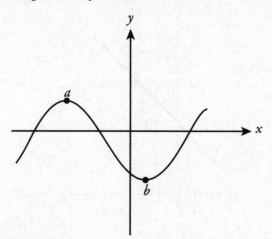

At $x < a$, $f(x)$ is rising.

At $a < x < b$, $f(x)$ is falling.

At $b < x$, $f(x)$ is rising again.

If a new function, $g(x)$, is formed by moving our original function $f(x)$, $g(x)$ would be defined as follows:

If $f(x)$ is moved 4 units up the y-axis, then $g(x) = f(x) + 4$.

If $f(x)$ is moved 5 units down the y-axis, then $g(x) = f(x) - 5$.

If $f(x)$ is moved 2 units to the right along the x-axis, then $g(x) = f(x - 2)$.

If $f(x)$ is moved 3 units up the y-axis, then $g(x) = f(x + 3)$.

Another aspect of functions that may be tested is the form in which they are written. For parabolas, you are probably used to the standard form, which is $ax^2 + bx + c = 0$. We've also factored quadratics, such as $(x - 2)(x + 5) = 0$ to find the roots of the parabola, or the places where it crosses the x-axis. Now let's talk about the vertex form of a parabola, which reveals the maximum or minimum value of a quadratic.

> In the vertex form, $f(x) = a(x - h)^2 + k$, the vertex is (h, k).

Knowing this form can make short work of a question that would be tough without it.

$$g(x) = (x - 5)(x + 3)$$

Which of the following is an equivalent form of the function g above in which the minimum value of g appears as a constant or coefficient?

A) $g(x) = x^2 - 15$

B) $g(x) = x^2 - 2x - 15$

C) $g(x) = (x - 1)^2 - 16$

D) $g(x) = (x + 1)^2 - 12$

Solution: There are a few opportunities to use POE here. The question asks for the minimum value, which is the vertex of the parabola. Only (C) and (D) are in vertex form, so (A) and (B) can be eliminated. To find out which one is correct, start by multiplying out the factors in the function using FOIL to get $g(x) = x^2 + 3x - 5x - 15 = x^2 - 2x - 15$. If you hadn't already eliminated (B), it would be a tempting choice at this point, since it is equivalent, but it's out of the running. From here, you could FOIL out (C) and (D) to see which is equivalent to the given function, or you could graph g and the remaining answers on your calculator to find a match. Knowing how to complete the square to convert a function to the vertex form will be necessary on some questions, though, so let's try that here. First, move the constants over to the other side to get $15 = x^2 - 2x$. Take half the coefficient on the x term, square it, and add it to both sides to get $15 + 1 = x^2 - 2x + 1$. The left side can be simplified and the right side written in square form, so the function becomes. $16 = (x - 1)^2$. Move the constant on the left back over to the other side to get $0 = (x - 1)^2 - 16$, which is (C).

QUICK QUIZ #7

Easy

11

t	−1	0	1	2
$g(t)$	0	−2	0	6

The table above provides values for the function g for selected values of t. Which of the following defines the function g?

A) $g(t) = t^2 - 2$

B) $g(t) = t^2 + 2$

C) $g(t) = 2t^2 - 2$

D) $g(t) = 2t^2 + 2$

Medium

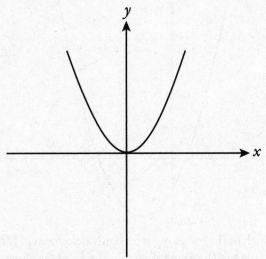

The quadratic function $y = f(x)$ is shown above.
Which of the following graphs represents the function
$y = f(x + 3) - 4$?

A)

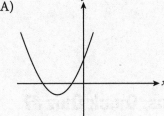

B)

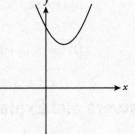

C)

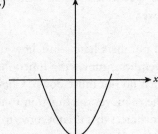

D)

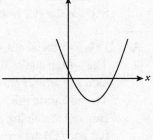

Hard

29

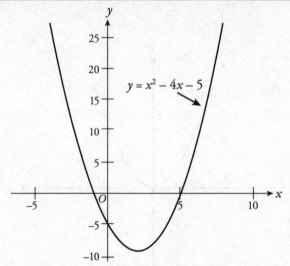

$y = x^2 - 4x - 5$

Which of the following is an equivalent form of the equation of the graph shown in the *xy*-plane above, from which the coordinates of vertex *Z* can be identified as constants in the equation?

A) $x(x - 4) - 5$

B) $(x - 2)^2 - 9$

C) $(x + 5)(x - 1)$

D) $(x - 5)(x + 1)$

Answers and Explanations: Quick Quiz #7

6. **C** Plug the values in the chart into the answer choices. Start with the easiest value for *t*, namely 0. Because when *t* is 0, $g(t)$ is –2, eliminate (B) and (D). Now check $t = 1$, which should yield $g(t) = 0$. Eliminate (A). Choice (C) is the answer.

18. **A** Don't worry about actual numbers here—just how the graph moves. The –4 outside of the parentheses moves the function down, so eliminate any answer choices that do not move down. Choice (B) is wrong. The +3 inside the parentheses moves the function to the left, so eliminate any remaining answer choices that do not move to the left. Choices (C) and (D) are wrong. Only (A) works.

29. **B** There are many chances to eliminate answers here, depending on what you see first. You may see there is a root at $x = 5$, so $(x - 5)$ must be one of the factors, eliminating (C). You may see that the equation must be in vertex form, and only (B) is in that form. You may also see from the graph that the vertex looks to be about $(2, -9)$, and only (B) has 2 and 9 in it. You could even graph the function on your calculator and see exactly what the vertex is. No matter how you get there, (B) is correct.

GEOMETRY: FINAL TIPS AND REMINDERS

- Always estimate first when the figure is drawn to scale.

- Always write the information given on the diagram, including any information you figure out along the way.

- If you don't know how to start, just look and see what shapes are involved. The solution to the problem will come through using the information we've gone over that pertains to that shape.

Chapter 5
Grid-In
Questions

GRID-INS

We've seen a few grid-in questions in the Quick Quizzes, so let's now take this time to focus on them. There will be 5 grid-ins at the end of Section 3 and 8 at the end of Section 4. The last two questions in Section 4 may be a pair of grid-ins based on the same information. Grid-in questions have no answer choices. You must solve the question, write your answer on a grid, and bubble it in. This isn't as bad as it sounds. Just as with the rest of the questions, there's a loosely ordered group of easy, medium, and hard grid-ins. Take your time on the easy and medium ones, as always.

Tips for Grid-In Happiness

- Don't bother to reduce fractions if they fit in the grid: $\frac{3}{6}$ is as good as $\frac{1}{2}$.

- Don't round off decimals. If your answer has more than four digits, just start to the left of the decimal point and fit in as many as you can.

- Don't grid in mixed fractions. Either convert to a mixed number or a decimal. (Use 4.25 or $\frac{17}{4}$, not $4\frac{1}{4}$.)

- If the question asks for "one possible value," any answer that works is okay.

- Forget about negatives, variables, and π. You can't grid them.

- You can still Plug In if the question has an implied variable.

QUICK QUIZ #1

Easy

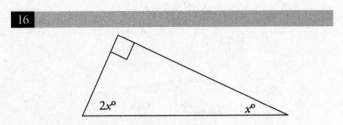

16

What is the value of x ?

Medium

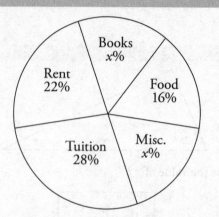

The chart above shows Orwell's projected expenditures for his freshman year at River State University. If he plans to spend a total of $10,000 for the year, how many dollars will Orwell spend on books?

Hard

If the function $r(s)$ is defined as $2s + 3$ for all values of s and $r(4) = x$, what is the value of $r(x)$?

Answers and Explanations: Quick Quiz #1

16. **30**   Since this is a right triangle, the other 2 angles add up to 90. So $3x = 90$ and $x = 30$.

34. **1700**   There are two steps: First, figure out the percentage of the budget spent on books. Then calculate the actual amount. All the pie slices add up to 100%, so $28 + 16 + 22 + 2x = 100$. $2x = 34$ and $x = 17\%$. Take 17% of 10,000, which is 1,700.

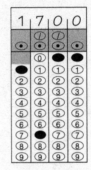

19. **25**   When a number is inside the parentheses, plug it into the equation. Thus, $r(4) = 2(4) + 3 = 11$, so $x = 11$. The question is not asking for $r(4)$, but $r(x)$. As you know $x = 11$, the question is asking for $r(11)$, so plug 11 into the formula: $r(11) = 2(11) + 3 = 25$.

Chapter 6
Problem Sets

The following groups of questions were designed for quick, concentrated study. The problems come in groups of ten and have a full range of difficulty. Answers and explanations follow immediately. The idea is for you to check your answers right after working the problems so that you can learn from your mistakes before you continue.

Don't simply count up how many you got wrong and then breeze on to the next thing—take a careful look at *how* you got the question wrong. Did you use the wrong strategy? Not remember the necessary basic math? Make a goofy computation error? Write an equation and Plug In at the same time?

> You need to know the cause of your mistakes before you can stop making them.

Here are sets of plugging in, geometry, exponent, and other typical problem types to help you learn how to recognize those types of questions when they come up—so pay attention to the look and feel of them.

One last thing—the question numbers here do not reflect the exact place the questions might appear on a real test. They are simply numbered 1 through 10. Since there's a loose order of difficulty on the test, you cannot count on the first third of a given section to be easy or the last third to be hard. You need to use your Personal Order of Difficulty to decide how to best spend your time.

PROBLEM SET 1: PLUGGING IN

Easy

1

Sinéad has 4 more than three times the number of hats that Maria has. If Maria has x hats, then in terms of x, how many hats does Sinéad have?

A) $3x + 4$

B) $3(x + 4)$

C) $4(x + 3)$

D) $4(3x)$

2

When 6 is subtracted from 10*p*, the result is *t*. Which of the following equations represents the statement above?

A) $t = 6(p - 10)$

B) $t = 6p - 10$

C) $t = 10(6 - p)$

D) $10p - 6 = t$

3

Sally scored a total of $4b + 12$ points in a certain basketball game. She scored the same number of points in each of the game's 4 periods. In terms of *b*, how many points did she score in each period?

A) $b + 3$

B) $b + 12$

C) $4b + 3$

D) $16b + 48$

Medium

4

$$v = \frac{1}{2}at^2$$

The velocity, *v*, of an object *t* seconds after beginning to accelerate from rest at a constant acceleration, *a*, can be found using the equation above. According to the formula, what is the ratio of the velocity of the object *t* seconds after the object begins to accelerate to the velocity of the object 2.5*t* seconds after the object begins to accelerate?

A) $\frac{4}{25}$

B) $\frac{2}{5}$

C) $\frac{5}{2}$

D) $\frac{25}{4}$

5

Roseanne is 6 years younger than Tom will be in 2 years. Roseanne is now x years old. In terms of x, how old was Tom 3 years ago?

A) $x - 7$

B) $x - 1$

C) $x + 1$

D) $x + 3$

6

A phone company charges 10 cents per minute for the first 3 minutes of a call and $10 - c$ cents for each minute thereafter. What is the cost, in cents, of a 10-minute phone call?

A) $100c + 70$

B) $30 + 7c$

C) $100 - 7c$

D) $100 - 70c$

7

If $0 < pt < 1$ and p is a negative integer, which of the following must be less than -1 ?

A) p

B) $p - t$

C) $t + p$

D) $2t$

Hard

8

If x and y are positive integers and $\sqrt{x} = y = 3$, then what is the value of y^2 ?

A) $x - 9$

B) $x + 9$

C) $x - 6\sqrt{x} + 9$

D) $x^2 - 6\sqrt{x} + 9$

If cupcakes are on sale at 8 for c cents, and gingerbread squares are on sale at 6 for g cents, what is the cost, in cents, of 2 cupcakes and 1 gingerbread square?

A) $8c + 3g$

B) $\dfrac{8c + 6g}{3}$

C) $\dfrac{8c + 3g}{14}$

D) $\dfrac{3c + 2g}{12}$

If the side of a square is $x + 1$, which of the following is the value of the diagonal of the square?

A) $x^2 + 1$

B) $x\sqrt{2} + \sqrt{2}$

C) $x^2 + 2$

D) $\sqrt{2x} + \sqrt{2}$

ANSWERS AND EXPLANATIONS: PROBLEM SET 1

Easy

1. **A** Forget the algebra. Plug in 2 for x, so Maria has 2 hats. Triple that number is 6. Sinéad has 4 more than triple, so Sinéad has $4 + 6 = 10$. You should put a circle around 10, so you can remember it's the answer to the question, the target number. Now plug 2 into the answer choices. Choice (A) gives you $3(2) + 4 = 10$, which matches the target, so keep (A). Choice (B) gives you $3(2 + 4) = 18$, which doesn't match the target, so eliminate (B). Choice (C) gives you $4(2 + 3)$, which doesn't match the target, so eliminate (C). Choice (D) is $4(3(2))$, which doesn't match the target, so eliminate (D). The answer is (A).

2. **D** Plug in 2 for p: $2 \times 10 = 20$ and $20 - 6 = 14$. So $t = 14$. (Since this is an equation, when you pick one number, the other number is auto-matically produced by the equation.) If $p = 2$ and $t = 14$, (A) is $14 = 6(2 - 10)$. Does $14 = 12 - 60$? Not on this planet. Choice (B) is $14 = 6(2) - 10$. This is false, so eliminate (B). Choice (C) is $14 = 10(6 - 2)$. This is false, so eliminate (C). Choice (D) is $10(2) - 6 = 14$, or $20 - 6 = 14$. The equation works, so that's your answer.

3. **A**   Make $b = 2$. That means she scored $4(2) + 12 = 20$ points total. If she scored the same number of points in each of the 4 periods, you have to divide the total by 4, so she scored $20 \div 4 = 5$ points per period. Put a circle around 5. Now on to the answer choices. Choice (A) is $2 + 3 = 5$, which is the target number. Choice (B) is $2 + 12 = 14$, so eliminate (B). Choice (C) is $4(2) + 3 = 11$, so eliminate (C). Choice (D) is $16(2) + 48 = 80$, so eliminate (D). The answer is (A).

> Notice how we keep plugging in 2? That's because we're trying to make things as easy as possible. To get these questions right, you didn't have to pick 2; on some questions, 2 might not work so well. You can pick whatever you want. Just make sure your number doesn't require you to make ugly, unpleasant calculations. Avoiding hard work is the name of the game. If the number you pick turns bad on you, pick another one.

> Always check all four answers when you plug in, just in case you get two correct answers. In that case, quickly plug in a new number to find out which one was wrong.

Medium

4. **A**   There are variables in the answer choices, so Plug In. Make $t = 2$. The question asks for the ratio of the velocity t (or 2) seconds after the object begins to accelerate to the velocity of the object $2.5t$ (or $2.5 \times 2 = 5$) seconds after it begins to accelerate. The velocity 2 seconds after the object begins to accelerate is $\frac{1}{2}a(2)^2 = 2a$. The velocity 5 seconds after the object begins to accelerate is $\frac{1}{2}a(5)^2 = \frac{25a}{2}$. Therefore, the ratio is $\frac{2a}{\frac{25a}{2}}$. Dividing by a fraction is the same as multiplying by its reciprocal, so the ratio becomes $2a \cdot \frac{2}{25a} = \frac{4a}{25a} = \frac{4}{25}$. The answer is (A).

5. **C**   Let $x = 10$, so Roseanne is now 10 years old. That's 6 years younger than 16, so Tom must be 16 in 2 years, which makes him 14 now. The question asks for Tom's age 3 years ago; if he's 14 now, 3 years ago he was 11. Circle 11. In the answer choices, plug 10 in for x. Choice (A) is $10 - 3$. Nope. Choice (B) is $10 - 1$. Nope. Choice (C) is $10 + 1$. Yeah! Just to be sure, let's check (D): $10 + 3 = 13$. Nope. The answer is (C).

6. **C** Let $c = 8$. The first 3 minutes of the call would be $3(10)$, or 30 cents. The remaining minutes would be charged at $10 - 8$ cents, or 2 cents a minute. There are 7 minutes remaining, so $2 \times 7 = 14$. The total cost is $30 + 14 = 44$ cents. On to the answer choices: (A) is way too big. Choice (B) is $30 + 7(8) = 86$. Choice (C) is $100 - 56 = 44$. The answer is (C).

7. **C** First, take a good look at $0 < pt < 1$. You know that pt is a positive fraction. If p is a negative integer, then t must be a negative fraction. Now Plug In. (Or you can just try numbers until you find some that satisfy the inequality.) Let $p = -1$ and $t = -\frac{1}{2}$. Try them in the answer choices, crossing out any answer that's -1 or higher. Choice (A) is -1, so cross it out. Choice (B) is $-\frac{1}{2}$, so cross it out. Choice (C) is $-1\frac{1}{2}$, so leave it in. Choice (D) is -1, so cross it out. The trouble with *must be* questions is that you can only *eliminate* answers by plugging in, you can't simply choose the first answer that works. That's because the answer may work with certain numbers but not with others—and you're looking for an answer that *must be true*, no matter what numbers you pick. These questions can be time-consuming, so if you're running low on time, you may want to skip them.

Hard

8. **C** Let $x = 25$. That makes $y = 2$. The question asks for y^2, and $2^2 = 4$. Circle it. Now try the answer choices. Choice (A) is $25 - 9$. Choice (B) is $25 + 9$. Choice (C) is $25 - 30 + 9 = 4$. Choice (D) is also huge. The answer is (C).

9. **D** Let $c = 16$ and $g = 12$. That means the cupcakes and the gingerbread squares sell for 2 cents apiece. One gingerbread square and two cupcakes will cost 6 cents. Circle 6. On to the answer choices, plugging in 16 for c and 12 for g. Choice (A) is $8(16) + 3(12)$, which is a lot bigger than 6. Choice (B) is $\frac{8(16) + 6(12)}{3} = \frac{200}{3}$, which is not 6. Choice (C) is $\frac{8(16) + 3(12)}{14} = \frac{164}{14}$, which is not 6. Choice (C)

gives you $2^2 + 2 = 4 + 2 = 6$, so eliminate it. Choice (D) gives you

$\dfrac{3(16) + 2(12)}{12} = 6$. Use your calculator for that last part. Get it right?

Then go to a bakery and celebrate.

10. **B**   Draw yourself a little square and label the sides $x + 1$. Draw in a diagonal. Let $x = 2$. The side of the square is then 3, and the diagonal is $3\sqrt{2}$. (The diagonal is the hypotenuse of a 45-45-90 triangle.) Plug 2 into the answer choices. Choice (A) gives you $2^2 + 1 = 5$. Eliminate (A). Choice (B) gives you $2\sqrt{2} + \sqrt{2} = 3\sqrt{2}$, so keep it and check the remaining answers. Choice (C) gives you $2^2 + 2 = 4 + 2 = 6$, so eliminate it. Choice (D) gives you $\sqrt{2(2)} + \sqrt{2} = 2 + \sqrt{2}$, so eliminate (D). The answer is (B).

PROBLEM SET 2: MORE PLUGGING IN

Easy

1

Jim and Pam bought x quarts of ice cream for a party. If 10 people attended the party, including Jim and Pam, and if each person ate the same amount of ice cream, which of the following represents the amount of ice cream, in quarts, eaten by each person at the party?

A) $10x$

B) $5x$

C) $\dfrac{x}{5}$

D) $\dfrac{x}{10}$

2

Addison has a reading assignment to complete. The number of pages he has left to read d days after being given the assignment can be modeled by the equation $n = 252 - 47d$, where n is the number of pages left to read. What is the meaning of 252 in the equation?

A) Addison reads 252 pages per day.

B) Addison reads 252 pages per hour.

C) Addison's book contains 252 pages.

D) Addison will complete the book in 252 days.

3

If $3x - y = 12$, which of the following is equivalent to $\dfrac{y}{3}$?

A) $x - 4$

B) $3x - 4$

C) $9x - 12$

D) $3x + 4$

Medium

4

When x is divided by 3, the remainder is z. In terms of z, which of the following could be equal to x ?

A) $z - 3$

B) $3 - z$

C) $3z$

D) $6 + z$

5

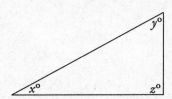

In the figure above, $2x = y$. Which of the following is equivalent to z ?

A) $180 + 2x$

B) $180 + x$

C) $180 - 3x$

D) $180 - 4x$

6

The 2005 to 2015 population density of a certain town can be modeled by the equation $d = 21.3y + 1,927.3$, where y represents the number of years since 2005 and d represents the population density. Which of the following best describes the meaning of the number 21.3 in the equation?

A) The estimated difference between the population density in 2005 and 2015

B) The estimated increase in the population density each year

C) The population density in 2005

D) The total population in 2005

7

The volume of a certain rectangular solid is $12x$. If the dimensions of the solid are the integers x, y, and z, what is the greatest possible value of z?

A) 24

B) 12

C) 6

D) 4

Hard

8

If $r = \dfrac{6}{3s + 2}$ and $tr = \dfrac{2}{3s + 2}$, what is the value of t?

A) $\dfrac{1}{4}$

B) $\dfrac{1}{3}$

C) 3

D) 4

When *a* is divided by 7, the remainder is 4. When *b* is divided by 3, the remainder is 2. If $0 < a < 24$ and $2 < b < 8$, which of the following could have a remainder of 0 when divided by 8 ?

A) $\dfrac{a}{b}$

B) $\dfrac{b}{a}$

C) $a + b$

D) ab

If $3x$, $\dfrac{3}{x}$, and $\dfrac{15}{x}$ are integers, which of the following must also be an integer?

  I. $\dfrac{x}{3}$

  II. x

  III. $6x$

A) II only

B) III only

C) I and III only

D) I, II, and III

ANSWERS AND EXPLANATIONS: PROBLEM SET 2

Easy

1. **D**   Plug in 20 for *x*. If 10 people eat 20 quarts, and they all eat the same amount, then each person eats 2 quarts. Put a circle around 2. Go to the answers and remember that $x = 20$. Choice (A) = $10 \times 20 = 200$. Nope. Choice (B) = $5 \times 20 = 100$. Nope. Choice (C) = $\dfrac{20}{5} = 4$. Nope. Choice (D) = $\dfrac{20}{10} = 2$. Yep.

2. **C** The question asks for the meaning of 252 in the equation. Go through each choice one at a time. Choice (A) says that Addison reads 252 pages per day. To determine the number of pages he reads per day, plug in $d = 1$ and $d = 2$ and look at the difference in n. If $d = 1$, then $n = 252 - 47(1) = 205$. If $d = 2$, then $n = 252 - 47(2) = 252 - 94 = 158$. The difference is $205 - 158 = 47$, so Addison reads 47 pages per day. Eliminate (A). Choice (B) says that Addison reads 252 pages per hour. No information is given about hours. Furthermore, the work done on (A) reveals that he reads fewer than 252 pages per day, so he must read less than that per hour. Eliminate (B). Choice (C) says that the book Addison is reading contains 252 pages. The number of pages in the book is the total number of pages that Addison has to read. Therefore, this is the number of pages that Addison has left to read after $d = 0$ days. Plug in $d = 0$ and see if $n = 252$. If $d = 0$, then $n = 252 - 47(0) = 252$. This is consistent with (C), so keep it. Choice (D) says that Addison will complete the book in 252 days. If that is the case, then when $d = 252$, n should be 0. Plug in $d = 252$ to get $n = 252 - 47(252)$. This is clearly less than 0, so eliminate (D). The answer is (C).

3. **A** Plug in 5 for x, which makes $y = 3$. So $\frac{y}{3} = \frac{3}{3} = 1$. Circle 1. On to the answers, and plug in $x = 5$. Choice (A) $= 5 - 4 = 1$. Keep (A). Choice (B) $= 3(5) - 4 = 11$. Eliminate (B). Choice (C) $= 9(5) - 12 = 33$. Eliminate (C). Choice (D) $= 3(5) + 4 = 19$. Eliminate (D). The answer is (A).

Why do we keep saying "circle it" in the explanations? Because that's the arithmetic answer to the question. All that's left to do is plug in for the variables in the answer choices, and look for your circled number. We tell you to circle that number so that it won't get lost in the shuffle and you can keep track of what you're doing.

Notice how sometimes, as in Question 2, you may have to plug in more than one set of numbers. That doesn't mean you're doing anything wrong, it's just the nature of the question. It also tends to happen on *must be* questions.

Also remember that you are trying to find numbers to plug in that make getting an answer to the question easy—so in Question 3, if we'd plugged in $x = 2$, that would've made y negative. Who wants to deal with negatives if they don't have to? If some kind of nastiness happens, bail out and *pick new numbers*.

Medium

4. **D**   Let $x = 7$ so $z = 1$. Try the answers. Choice (A) is $z - 3$, or $1 - 3 = -2$. Nope. Choice (B) is $3 - z$ or $3 - 1 = 2$. Nope. Choice (C) is $3z$, or $3(1) = 3$. Nope. Choice (D) is $6 + z$, or $6 + 1 = 7$. Yep, that's correct!

5. **C**   Plug in 10 for x, which makes $y = 20$. Remember that a triangle has 180°, so the third angle, z, must equal $180 - 30 = 150$. Circle 150. Try the answers, with $x = 10$. Choice (A) gives you $180 + 2(10) = 200$. No. Choice (B) gives you $180 + 10 = 190$. No. Choice (C) gives you $180 - 30 = 150$, which is what you're looking for. Choice (D) gives you $180 - 4(10) = 140$. No. The answer is (C).

6. **B**   The question asks for the meaning of 21.3 in the equation. Go through each choice and determine whether each is 21.3. Choice (A) is the estimated difference between the population density in 2005 and 2015. Since y represents the years since 2005, $y = 0$ for 2005 and $y = 10$ for 2015. To determine the difference in population density between 2005 and 2015, plug in $y = 0$ and $y = 10$. If $y = 0$, then $d = 21.3(0) + 1{,}927.3 = 1{,}927.3$ If $y = 10$, then $d = 21.3(10) + 1{,}927.3 = 2{,}140.3$. The difference is $2{,}140.3 - 1927.3 = 213$. The difference is not 21.3, so eliminate (A). Choice (B) is the estimated increase in population density each year. To determine whether this is 21.3, plug in $y = 0$ and $y = 1$ and look at the increase in d. If $y = 0$, then $d = 21.3(0) + 1{,}927.3 = 1{,}927.3$. If $y = 1$, then $d = 21.3(1) + 1{,}927.3 = 1{,}948.6$. The increase is $1948.6 - 1927.3 = 21.3$. This is consistent with the target, so keep (B). Choice (C) is the population density in 2005. This is represented by the value of d, when $y = 0$, which is 1,927.3, so eliminate (C). Choice (D) is the total population. The equation only models population density, not total population. In order to determine total population, the area of the town would be needed. This information is not given, so total population cannot be determined. Eliminate (D). The answer is (B).

7. **B**   First, draw yourself a picture. (Think shoebox.) Plug in 2 for x. The formula for volume of a rectangular solid is length × width × height—in this case, xyz. The volume is $12x = 12(2) = 24$. Now come up with 3 different numbers—2 is one of them—that result in a total of 24 when multiplied together.

A chart is never a bad idea. It keeps you organized.

x	y	z
2	1	12

Since y is as low as possible, z is as big as possible. Go with it. If you're not convinced, try other combinations—but don't forget, the question asks for the greatest possible value of z.

Hard

8. **B** Both equations have s in them, so plug in a value for s, such as 2. If

$s = 2$, $r = \dfrac{6}{3(2) + 2} = \dfrac{6}{8}$. Now plug the values for s and r into the second

equation to get $t\left(\dfrac{6}{8}\right) = \dfrac{2}{3(2) + 2}$ or $\dfrac{6t}{8} = \dfrac{2}{8}$. Therefore, $6t = 2$ and $t = \dfrac{1}{3}$.

The answer is (B).

9. **C** Plug in 11 for a and 5 for b. Those two choices satisfy all the conditions of the problem. Check the answers: (A) is a fraction; forget about it. Choice (B) is $11 - 5 = 6$, which isn't divisible by 8. Choice (C) gives you $11 + 5 = 16$. If you divide 16 by 8, you get a quotient of 2 and a remainder of 0. End of story.

10. **B** How about plugging in 3 for x? Try the answers—you're looking for integers, so if the answer isn't an integer, you can cross it out.

I. $\dfrac{x}{3} = \dfrac{3}{3} = 1$ OK so far.

II. $x = 3$ OK so far.

III. $6x = 6 \bullet 3 = 18$.   OK so far.

At this point, your average test taker figures the question is pretty easy and picks (D). Not you, my friend. *This is a hard question.* You must go an extra step. Plug in a new number. Since the question concerns integers, what if you plug in something that isn't an integer, like $x = \dfrac{1}{3}$?

I. $\dfrac{\frac{1}{3}}{3} = \dfrac{1}{9}$.   That's no integer. Cross it out.

II. $\dfrac{1}{3}$.   No good either.

III. $6\left(\dfrac{1}{3}\right) = 2$.   Okay.

Since you have eliminated I and II, only III remains.

PROBLEM SET 3: PLUGGING IN THE ANSWER CHOICES

Easy

1

If x is a positive integer, and $x + 12 = x^2$, what is the value of x ?

A) 2

B) 4

C) 6

D) 12

2

If twice the sum of three consecutive numbers is 12, and the two lowest numbers add up to 3, what is the highest number?

A) 2

B) 3

C) 6

D) 9

3

If $2^x = 8^{(x-4)}$, what is the value of x ?

A) 4

B) 6

C) 8

D) 64

Medium

4

If Jane bought 3 equally priced shirts on sale, she would have 2 dollars left over. If instead she bought 10 equally priced pairs of socks, she would have 7 dollars left over. If the prices of both shirts and socks are integers, which of the following, in dollars, could be the amount that Jane has to spend?

A) 28

B) 32

C) 47

D) 57

During a vacation together, Bob spent twice as much as Josh, who spent four times as much as Ralph. If Bob and Ralph together spent $180, how much did Josh spend?

A) $20

B) $80

C) $120

D) $160

Tina has half as many marbles as Louise. If Louise gave away 3 of her marbles and lost 2 more, she would have 1 more marble than Tina. How many marbles does Tina have?

A) 3

B) 5

C) 6

D) 7

In a bag of jellybeans, $\frac{1}{3}$ are cherry and $\frac{1}{4}$ are licorice. If the remaining 20 jellybeans are orange, how many jellybeans are in the bag?

A) 16

B) 32

C) 36

D) 48

Hard

If the circumference of a circle is equal to twice its area, which of the following is equal to the area of this circle?

A) π

B) 2π

C) 4π

D) 16π

9

If $12y = x^3$, and x and y are positive integers, what is the least possible value for y?

A) 6

B) 18

C) 144

D) 216

10

If x^2 is added to $\dfrac{5}{4y}$, the sum is $\dfrac{5+y}{4y}$. If y is a positive integer, which of the following is the value of x?

A) $\dfrac{1}{4}$

B) $\dfrac{1}{2}$

C) $\dfrac{4}{5}$

D) 1

ANSWERS AND EXPLANATIONS: PROBLEM SET 3

Easy

1. **B**   Start with (C), $6 = x$. That gives you $6 + 12 = 36$. No good. At this point, don't stare at the other choices, waiting for divine inspiration—just pick another one and try it. It's okay if the next answer you try isn't right either. If you plug in 4 for x, you get $4 + 12 = 16$. The equation is true, so that's that.

2. **B**   Start with (C). If the highest number is 6, the other two are 5 and 4. 5 and 4 don't add up to 3—cross out (C). Try (B). If the highest number is 3, the other two numbers are 1 and 2. (They have to be consecutive.) The sum of $3 + 2 + 1 = 6$, and twice the sum of $6 = 12$. If you picked (A), you didn't pay attention to what the question asked for. Be sure to reread the question so you know which number they want.

3. **B**   Try (C) first. Does $2^8 = 8^4$? Nope. (Use your calculator.) Try something lower, like (B). Does $2^6 = 8^2$? Yes.

Medium

4. **C**   Try (C) first. If Jane has $47 to spend, 47 ÷ 3 = 15 with 2 left over. (The shirts cost $15 apiece.) Now try 47 ÷ 10 = 4, with 7 left over. (Socks are $4 a pair.) It works.

5. **B**   Try (C) first. If Josh spent $120, Bob spent $240 and Ralph spent $40. That means Bob and Ralph together spent $280, not $180 as the problem states. Choice (C) is no good. Since (C) was way too big, try something smaller. If Josh spent $80, Bob spent $160 and Ralph spent $20. So Bob and Ralph together spent $180. That's more like it.

6. **C**   Start with (B). If Tina has 5 marbles, then Louise has 10. If Louise gives away 3, then she has 7. If she loses 2 more, she's down to 5. You're supposed to end up with Louise having 1 more than Tina, but they both have 5. Cross out (B)—and you know you're close to the right answer. Try (C). If Tina has 6, Louise has 12. If Louise gives away and loses 5, she's got 7, which is 1 more than Tina has.

7. **D**   Try (B) first. Oops—$\frac{1}{3}$ of 32 is a fraction. Forget (B). Try (C): $\frac{1}{3}$ of 36 = 12 and $\frac{1}{4}$ of 36 = 9. Does 12 + 9 + 20 = 36? No. Try (D). $\frac{1}{3}$ of 48 = 16 and $\frac{1}{4}$ of 48 = 12. Does 16 + 12 + 20 = 48? Yes!

Making a simple chart will help you keep track of your work:

	C	D
cherry	12	16
licorice	9	12
orange	20	20
TOTAL	41	48

Hard

8. **A** Try (B) first. If the area is 2π, then the radius becomes a fraction. That's probably not going to be the answer, so you should move on. Try (A). If the area is π, then the radius is 1 ($\pi r^2 = \pi$, $r^2 = 1$, $r = 1$). If $r = 1$, the circumference is $2\pi(1) = 2\pi$. So the circumference is twice the area. Beautiful.

9. **B** Solve this problem with a combination of factoring and Plugging In. The question looks like this: $2 \times 2 \times 3y = x^3$. Now factor the answer choices, starting with the smallest one, as the question asks for the least possible value of y. Choice (A) is $3 \bullet 2$. If you plug that in for y, does it give you a cube? Nope. Choice (B) is $2 \times 3 \times 3$—now you have $(2 \times 3)(2 \times 3)(2 \times 3) = x^3$. It works.

10. **B** Choice (C) is particularly nasty here, so try (B) first. This gives you

$\dfrac{1}{4} + \dfrac{5}{4y}$. When these fractions are added together, the sum is $\dfrac{5 + y}{4y}$,

which matches what the question is looking for. You could also solve by

plugging in—choose a positive integer for y, plug it into the equation,

and see what happens. You end up with $x = \dfrac{1}{2}$.

> When you Plug In, start with the easier of the two middle choices, as you hopefully did for Question 10. Don't worry if you have to try a couple of answer choices before you hit the right one—the first one you do is always the slowest, because you're still finding your way. Subsequent tries should be easier, and in most cases, it's still likely to be easier than writing out equations.

PROBLEM SET 4: MORE PLUGGING IN THE ANSWER CHOICES

Easy

1

If $\frac{a-4}{28} = \frac{1}{4}$, what is the value of a ?

A) 11

B) 10

C) 7

D) 6

2

If the area of $\triangle ABC$ is 21, and the length of the height minus the length of the base equals 1, which of the following is equal to the base of the triangle?

A) 2

B) 4

C) 6

D) 7

3

If $d^2 = \sqrt{4} + d + 10$, what is the value of d ?

A) 2

B) 3

C) 4

D) 16

Medium

4

If $\frac{4}{x-1} = \frac{x+1}{2}$, which of the following is a possible value of x ?

A) −1

B) 1

C) 2

D) 3

$$f(x) = \dfrac{1}{(x-3)^2 - 6(x-3) + 9}$$

For what value of x is the function f defined above undefined?

A) -6

B) -3

C) 3

D) 6

If $16{,}000 = 400(x + 9)$, what is the value of x ?

A) 391

B) 310

C) 40

D) 31

What is the radius of a circle with an area of $\dfrac{\pi}{4}$?

A) 0.2

B) 0.4

C) 0.5

D) 2.0

Hard

If 20 percent of x is 36 less than x percent of $x - 70$, what is the value of x ?

A) 140

B) 120

C) 100

D) 50

If $x^2 = y^3$ and $(x - y)^2 = 2x$, then which of the following is a possible value of y ?

A) 64

B) 16

C) 8

D) 4

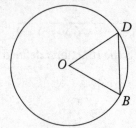

In the circle with center O, $OD = DB$ and arc $DB = 2\pi$.
What is the area of the circle?

A) 36π

B) 16π

C) 12π

D) 4π

ANSWERS AND EXPLANATIONS: PROBLEM SET 4

Easy

1. **A** Try (C) first. Does $\frac{3}{28} = \frac{1}{4}$? Nope. Look for a bigger number—(B) gives

   you $\frac{6}{28}$, which is closer, but still no cigar. Choice (A) gives you $\frac{7}{28} = \frac{1}{4}$.

2. **C** Try (B) first. If the base = 4, then $h - 4 = 1$ and $h = 5$. The formula for

   area of a triangle is $\frac{1}{2}bh$, so the area would be 10. Too small. Try (C). If

   the base is 6, then $h - 6 = 1$ and $h = 7$. The area is $\frac{42}{2} = 21$.

3. **C** Yes, it looks nasty, but it's a breeze with the miracle of Plugging In the

   Answers. Try (B) first: $3^2 = \sqrt{4} + 3 + 10$; $9 = 2 + 13$. Forget it. Try (C):

   $4^2 = 2 + 4 + 10$; $16 = 16$. That's it.

> If you try one of the middle choices and it doesn't work, take a second to see if
> you need a bigger or smaller number. But if you can't tell quickly, don't spend
> too much time thinking about it—just try one direction and keep going.

Medium

4. **D**   Try (B) first. If $x = 1$, does $\dfrac{4}{0}$ …forget it. You can't divide by 0. Try (C). If $x = 2$, does $\dfrac{4}{1} = \dfrac{3}{2}$? No way. Try (D). If $x = 3$, does $\dfrac{4}{2} = \dfrac{4}{2}$? Yes. Remember to avoid trying negatives [such as (A)] unless they're all you have left or you have some reason to think they'll be right.

5. **D**   The question asks for a specific value, and there are numbers in the answer choices. A fraction is undefined when the denominator is zero, so plug in the values to see which one makes $(x-3)^2 - 6(x-3) + 9 = 0$. Start with (C). When $x = 3$, the denominator becomes $(3-3)^2 - 6(3-3) + 9 = 0^2 - 6(0) + 9 = 9$. Eliminate (C). It may be hard to tell if you need a bigger number or a smaller one, so just pick a direction. For (D), if $x = 6$, the denominator becomes $(6-3)^2 - 6(6-3) + 9 = 3^2 - 6(3) + 9 = 9 - 18 + 9 = 0$. The answer is (D).

6. **D**   Try (C) first. Does $400 \cdot 49 = 16,000$? No, and hopefully you just estimate that and don't bother doing it, with or without your calculator. How about (D)? $400(40) = 16,000$. Yep. If you picked (A), you miscounted the zeros. Try checking your answers on your calculator.

7. **C**   This is a fabulous Plugging In question. Try (C) first. Convert 0.5 to a fraction, because fractions are better than decimals and because the question has a fraction in it. If the radius is $\dfrac{1}{2}$, the area is $\pi\left(\dfrac{1}{2}\right)^2 = \pi\left(\dfrac{1}{4}\right) = \dfrac{\pi}{4}$.

> **Why do we like fractions better than decimals?**
>
> Mostly because that irritating little decimal point is so easily misplaced. Also because decimals can get very tiny and hard to estimate. You don't want to convert decimals to fractions automatically—only when the question would be easier to do that way. If the question is in decimals and the answers are in decimals, then don't bother converting.

Hard

8. **B**   Try (C) first because the question is about percents and 100 is easy to do. 20% of 100 is 20. 100% of $100 - 70$ is 30. Does $30 - 20 = 46$? Nah. Try (B). 20% of 120 is 24. 120% of 50 is 60. Does $60 - 24 = 36$? Yes.

9. **D**   Try (C) first. If $y = 8$, then $x^2 = 8^3$. $8^3 = 512$. If $x^2 = 512$, x isn't an integer. Forget (C). Try (D). If $y = 4$, then $x^2 = 4^3$, $x^2 = 64$, and $x = 8$. Now try them in the second equation: $(8-4)^2 = 2(8)$. $4^2 = 16$. It works. Notice that when (C) didn't work, you went with a smaller number because it was easier.

10. **A** First, write in 2π beside arc *DB*. Now try (B). If the area is 16π, the radius is 4. Write in 4 beside the two radii, and also *DB*, because *OD* = *DB*. Aha! That makes triangle *DOB* equilateral! Since angle *DOB* is 60°, and $\frac{60}{360} = \frac{1}{6}$, that makes arc *DB* $\frac{1}{6}$ of the circumference. Remember our radius is 4, so the circumference is 8π. Uh oh—2π is not $\frac{1}{6}$ of 8π. So cross off (B). But at least now you know what to do. Try (A). If the area is 36π, the radius is 6 and the circumference is 12π. Is $\frac{1}{6}$ of 12π equal to 2π? Yeah! Did that seem really painful? It was a lot of work, but then, it was a hard question. The reason Plugging In is a good technique for this problem is that if you Plug In the Answers, you get to move through the question like a robot, one step after the other, and you don't have to depend on a flash of insight.

PROBLEM SET 5: ESTIMATING

Easy

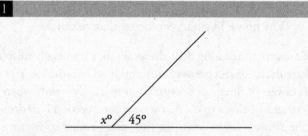

What is the value of $2x$?

A) 270

B) 135

C) 90

D) 67.5

2

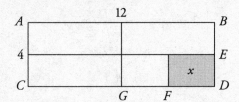

If *F* is equidistant from *G* and *D*, and *E* is equidistant from *B* and *D*, what fractional part of rectangle *ABDC* is area *x*?

A) $\frac{1}{16}$

B) $\frac{1}{8}$

C) $\frac{1}{4}$

D) $\frac{1}{2}$

3

If Sarah bought 12 pies for $30, how many pies could she have bought for $37.50 at the same rate?

A) 9

B) 12

C) 15

D) 24

Medium

4

If a runner completes one lap of a track in 64 seconds, approximately how many minutes will it take her to run 40 laps at the same speed?

A) 30

B) 43

C) 52

D) 128

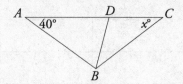

In the figure above, $BD = DC$ and $AB = AD$. What is the value of x ?

A) 110

B) 70

C) 55

D) 35

Martina wants to buy as many felt-tip pens as possible for $10. If the pens cost between $1.75 and $2.30, what is the greatest number of pens Martina can buy?

A) 4

B) 5

C) 6

D) 7

If 1.2 is p percent of 600, what is the value of p ?

A)   0.2%

B)   5%

C)   20%

D) 500%

Hard

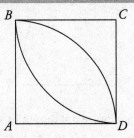

In the figure above, *ABCD* is a square with sides of 4. What is the length of arc *BD* ?

A) 8π

B) 4π

C) 2π

D) π

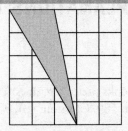

Each of the small squares in the figure above has an area of 4. If the shortest side of the triangle is equal in length to 2 sides of a small square, what is the area of the shaded triangle?

A) 40

B) 24

C) 20

D) 16

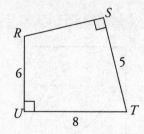

Note: Figure not drawn to scale.

In the figure above, what is the length of *RS* ?

A) 10

B) $5\sqrt{3}$

C) 8

D) $2\sqrt{3}$

ANSWERS AND EXPLANATIONS: PROBLEM SET 5

Easy

1. **A** Estimate first: *x* looks pretty big, doesn't it? Bigger than 90? Yes. So 2*x* will be bigger than 180. Cross out (B), (C), and (D). Only (A) remains.

2. **B** Use your eyeballs and compare against the answer choices. The horizontal line and the longer vertical line appear to divide the rectangle into four equal pieces. Since the shaded region is only part of one of those pieces, the answer is less than $\frac{1}{4}$. Eliminate (C) and (D). The shaded region appears to be about half of the piece. Therefore, the shaded region should be about half of a quarter, which is $\frac{1}{2} \cdot \frac{1}{4} = \frac{1}{8}$. It's also helpful to draw more boxes in the figure, and then you could count them up:

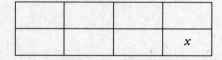

3. **C** \$37.50 is going to buy more pies than \$30, right? So cross out anything less than or equal to 12. Say goodbye to (A) and (B). Now, any chance an extra 7.50 will buy nearly another 12 pies? No. Eliminate (D).

Medium

4. **B** This is a great question for estimating. Don't like 64 seconds? Call it 60, or 1 minute. If the runner completes a lap in just over a minute, she'll complete 40 laps in just over 40 minutes. Only (B) is close.

5. **D** First, just eyeball the angle. It's smaller than 90°. It's close to angle *BAD*, which is marked 40. You're down to (C) and (D). Is it a little smaller than *BAD* or 15° bigger than *BAD*? Go for it! You can always come back and check your answer the long way if you have time.

   The long way: *BAD* is isosceles, since $AB = AD$. The two base angles of *BAD* = 140, so each is 70°. If $\angle BDA = 70°$, then $\angle BDC$ is 110°. Triangle *BDC* is isosceles too, with $\angle DCB$ and $\angle CBD = x°$. $2x = 70$, so $x = 35°$. Now admit it—isn't estimating easier?

6. **B** If Martina wants to buy as many pens as possible, she'll want to buy the cheaper pens, which cost a little less than $2. If the pens cost exactly $2, she can buy 5 pens for $10. Therefore, she can buy more than 4, so eliminate (A). Because the pens cost a little bit less than $2, it is possible that she can buy a little more than 5 pens. It won't be a lot more than 5, so eliminate (D). On medium questions, estimating may only get rid of one or two answers, so try the remaining ones. Test (C). If she buys 6 pens for $1.75, she will have to pay $6 \times \$1.75 = \$10.50$. Since this is more than $10, eliminate (C).

7. **A** Start by finding 10% of 600, which is 60. Since 1.2 is less than 60, the answer must be less than 10%. Eliminate (C) and (D). Now, 1% of 600 is 6. Since 1.2 is less than 6, the value of p must be less than 1%. Eliminate (B).

Hard

8. **C** First, mark the sides of the square with 4. Now estimate the length of *BD*, based on the side of the square. Think of the side of the square as a piece of spaghetti that you are going to drape over *BD*. So *BD* is longer than 4. *BD* is also shorter than the distance from *B* to *C* to *D*, which would be 8. Now go to the answers, and substitute 3 for π. (You know, $\pi = 3.14$, but you don't have to be so exact. You're just estimating.) Choice (A) is around 24. Way too big. Choice (B) is around 12, and (C) is around 6. Choice (D) is too small. Pick (C) and move on.

9. **C** When you estimate, remember that each shaded square has an area of 4. It's tricky to do this exactly, because mostly only slivers of squares are shaded. So estimate it. Almost 2 full squares at the top, another square on the next row (that's 3 so far) and then slivers on the next 3 rows that make up about 2 full squares. So you've got 5 squares each with area 4; the area of the triangle is around 20, so pick (C).

As an alternative, you can work out an exact answer. If each square has an area of 4, then the side of a little square is 2. Write that on the figure, in a couple of places. Now use the top of the triangle as the base. It equals 4. The other thing you need is the height, or altitude, of the triangle—and in this case, the height is equal to a side of the big square, or 10. Using the formula for the area of a triangle, plug 4 in for the base and 10 in for the height and you get 20 for the area.

10. **B**   Hey, wake up! You can't estimate anything if the figure isn't drawn to scale! But you may want to redraw the figure to make it look more like it's supposed to look. Now for the solution: Draw a line from R to T, slicing the figure into 2 triangles. Now all you have to do is use the Pythagorean Theorem to calculate the lengths. Triangle RUT is a 6:8:10 triangle, a Pythagorean triple. Now for RST: $a^2 + 5^2 = 10^2$. So $a^2 = 75$ and $a = 5\sqrt{3}$.

PROBLEM SET 6: FRACTIONS, DECIMALS, AND PERCENTS

Easy

1

A big-screen TV is on sale at 15% off the regular price. If the regular price of the TV is $420, what is the sale price?

A) $63

B) $357

C) $405

D) $483

2

Which of the following is the decimal form of $70 + \frac{7}{10} + \frac{3}{1,000}$?

A) 70.0703

B) 70.7003

C) 70.703

D) 70.73

3

If n is six more than two-thirds of twelve, what is the value of n?

A) 10

B) 12

C) 14

D) 18

Medium

4

Walking at a constant rate, Stuart takes 24 minutes to walk to the nearest bus stop and $\frac{1}{3}$ of that time to walk to the movie theater. It takes him half the time to walk to school than it does for him to walk to the movie theater. How many minutes does it take Stuart to walk to school?

A) 36

B) 24

C) 8

D) 4

5

What is the value of x if $\dfrac{\frac{1}{2}}{x} = 4$?

A) 8

B) 2

C) $\dfrac{1}{4}$

D) $\dfrac{1}{8}$

6

If $x\%$ of y is 10, which of the following is equal to $y\%$ of x ?

A) 1

B) 5

C) 10

D) 90

7

A certain drink is made by adding 4 parts water to 1 part drink mix. If the amount of water is doubled, and the amount of drink mix is quadrupled, what percent of the new mixture is drink mix?

A) $33\frac{1}{3}\%$

B) 50%

C) $66\frac{2}{3}\%$

D) 80%

Hard

8

Set A consists only of fractions with a numerator of 1 and a denominator d such that $1 < d < 8$, where d is an integer. If Set B consists of the reciprocals of the fractions with odd denominators in Set A, then what is the product of all the numbers that are elements of either Set A or Set B ?

A) $\frac{1}{96}$

B) $\frac{1}{48}$

C) $\frac{1}{24}$

D) 1

9

The function g is defined as $g(x) = \dfrac{x^2}{3 - |x - 4|}$.

For which values of x is $g(x)$ NOT defined?

A) $x = 4$ and $x = 7$

B) $x = 3$ and $x = 4$

C) $x = 3$ and $x = 7$

D) $x = 1$ and $x = 7$

If a, b, and c are distinct positive integers, and 10% of abc is 5, then which of the following is a possible value of $a + b$?

A) 3

B) 5

C) 8

D) 25

ANSWERS AND EXPLANATIONS: PROBLEM SET 6

Easy

1. **B** The numbers are too awkward to plug in, so do it the old-fashioned way: 15% of $420 is $0.15 \times 420 = 63$. $420 - 63 = 357$. Use your calculator.

2. **C** Take the pieces one at a time and eliminate. The first piece is 70. The second piece is $\frac{7}{10}$, or 0.7. Eliminate (A). The last piece is $\frac{3}{1,000}$, or 0.003. Eliminate (B) and (D).

3. **C** Translate the problem into math language: $n = 6 + \frac{2}{3} \times 12$. Then, don't forget PEMDAS: Multiply before you add. $n = 6 + \frac{2}{3}(12) = 6 + 8 = 14$.

Medium

4. **D** Start working from the 24 minutes it takes poor Stuart to walk to the bus stop. (Won't anybody give the guy a ride?) If it takes $\frac{1}{3}$ of 24 to walk to the movies, that's 8 minutes. If it takes him half of that time to walk to school, $\frac{1}{2}$ of 8 is 4. This question requires close reading more than anything else.

5. **D** Plugging In the Answers wouldn't be a bad idea here—you can eliminate (A) and (B) pretty quickly that way. Choice (C) is $\frac{\frac{1}{2}}{\frac{1}{4}} = 2$. Choice (D) is $\frac{\frac{1}{2}}{\frac{1}{8}} = 4$.

6. **C**   Plug in 10 for y, which makes $x = 100$. Plug those numbers into the second part: 100% of 10 = 10.

Alternatively, translate. The sentence x% of y is 10 translates to $\frac{x}{100} \cdot y = 10$. This simplifies to $\frac{xy}{100} = 10$. The expression y% of x translates to $\frac{y}{100} \cdot x$. This simplifies to $\frac{yx}{100} = \frac{xy}{100}$, which equals 10.

7. **A**   First, make a little chart: If you double the water and quadruple the mix, you get

water		mix
4	:	1
8	:	4

Reread the question. It asks for the percentage of the new mixture that's drink mix. You've got $\frac{4 \text{ (mix)}}{12 \text{ (total)}}$, which equals $\frac{1}{3}$, or $33\frac{1}{3}$%.

If you made it almost to the end but picked (B), don't forget that you have to express the mix as a percentage of the total, not a percentage of the water.

Hard

8. **B**   Read this carefully. Set A has different fractions, each with a numerator of 1. (You might as well write them down like that and fill in the denominators when you get there.) The denominators are between 1 and 8. That gives you Set A: $\frac{1}{2}, \frac{1}{3}, \frac{1}{4}, \frac{1}{5}, \frac{1}{6}, \frac{1}{7}$. Set B has the reciprocals of the members of Set A with odd denominators, so Set B: $\frac{3}{1}, \frac{5}{1}, \frac{7}{1}$. Now multiply all the elements together—see how the fractions that have reciprocals cancel each other out? You're left with $\frac{1}{2} \times \frac{1}{4} \times \frac{1}{6}$, which is $\frac{1}{48}$.

9. **D**   The function will not be defined when the denominator is equal to 0. If you don't want to analyze the denominator to determine when it would equal 0, you can Plug In the Answers. Even though the answers are not in ascending or descending order, you can still start with (C). If you plug 3 into the denominator, you do not get zero, so eliminate anything with a 3: (B) and (C). Notice that both of the remaining answers have 7, so there's no need to test it. Try 1 in (D). You get 0, so eliminate (A) and then pick (D).

10. **A**   First, translate the middle part of the problem into an equation. 10% of abc is 5 translates to $\frac{10}{100} \cdot abc = 5$. Now solve for abc and get $abc = 50$. Reread the question. Each variable is different, each is positive, and multiplied together they produce 50. Now Plug In the Answers, remembering that the answers represent $a + b$. In (A), $a + b$ would have to be 1 + 2. If $a = 1$ and $b = 2$ and $abc = 50$, what is c? $c = 25$, so it works.

A couple of reminders: If you are making mistakes on the easy and medium problems, don't spend a lot of time—if any—working on the hard problems. You need to hone your skills first; you may want to go back to the review section and do some work before continuing. And don't forget, you probably want to leave some questions blank on the real thing.

PROBLEM SET 7: AVERAGES, RATIOS, PROPORTIONS, AND PROBABILITIES

1

Three consecutive integers add up to 258. What is the smallest integer?

A) 58

B) 85

C) 86

D) 89

2

A factory produces 6,000 plates per day. If one out of 15 plates is broken, how many unbroken plates does the factory produce each day?

A) 5,800

B) 5,600

C) 800

D) 400

3

It takes 4 friends 24 minutes to wash all the windows in Maria's house. The friends all work at the same rate. How long would it take 8 friends, working at the same rate, to wash all the windows in Maria's house?

A) 48

B) 20

C) 12

D) 8

Medium

4

The value of t is inversely proportional to the value of w. If value of w increases by a factor of 5, what happens to the value of t ?

A) t increases by a factor of 5.

B) t increases by a factor of 2.

C) t decreases by a factor of 2.

D) t decreases by a factor of 5.

5

A drawer holds only blue socks and white socks. If the ratio of blue socks to white socks is 4:3, which of the following could be the total number of socks in the drawer?

A)   4

B)   7

C) 12

D) 24

6

The probability of choosing a caramel from a certain bag of candy is $\frac{1}{5}$, and the probability of choosing a butterscotch is $\frac{5}{8}$. If the bag contains 40 pieces of candy, and the only types of candy in the bag are caramel, butterscotch, and fudge, how many pieces of fudge are in the bag?

A)   5

B)   7

C)   8

D) 25

7

Dixie spent an average of x dollars on each of 5 shirts and an average of y dollars on each of 3 hats. In terms of x and y, how many dollars did she spend on shirts and hats?

A) $5x + 3y$

B) $15(x + y)$

C) $8xy$

D) $15xy$

Hard

8

If the ratio of $\frac{1}{6} : \frac{1}{5}$ is equal to the ratio of 35 to x, what is the value of x ?

A) 24

B) 30

C) 36

D) 42

9

An artist makes a certain shade of green paint by mixing blue and yellow in a ratio of 3:4. She makes orange by mixing red and yellow in a ratio of 2:3. If on one day she mixes both green and orange and uses equal amounts of blue and red paint, what fractional part of the paint that she uses is yellow?

A) $\frac{7}{12}$

B) $\frac{17}{29}$

C) $\frac{7}{5}$

D) $\frac{12}{17}$

10

The areas of two circles are in a ratio of 4:9. If both radii are integers, and $r_1 - r_2 = 2$, which of the following is the radius of the larger circle?

A) 4

B) 6

C) 8

D) 9

ANSWERS AND EXPLANATIONS: PROBLEM SET 7

Easy

1. **B**   If the three integers add up to 258, then their average is 258 ÷ 3, or 86. Since the integers are consecutive, they must be 85, 86, and 87. Check it on your calculator. If you picked (C), what did you do wrong? Forget what the question asked for? Divide 258 by 3 and then quit? Even easy problems may have more than one step. This would also be a good question in which to Plug In the Answers.

2. **B**   First, estimate. You're looking for the number of unbroken plates—if only one broke out of 15, there should be a lot of unbroken plates, right? Cross out (C) and (D). Now set up a proportion:

$$\frac{\text{broken}}{\text{total}} = \frac{1}{15} = \frac{x}{6,000}$$

Now cross-multiply. You get 6,000 = 15x, so using your calculator, x = 400. That's the number of broken plates, so subtract 400 from 6,000 and you've got the answer. If you picked (D), you could have gotten the problem right if you had either estimated first or reread the question right before you answered it.

3. **C**   There are twice as many people, so the work will go twice as fast. You can't set up a normal proportion because it's an inverse proportion—the more people you have, the less time the work takes. So if you multiply the number of people by 2, you divide the work time by 2.

Medium

4. **D**   Since no values were given, try plugging in values of your own to test what happens. If t starts out as 10 and w starts out as 5, you can set up the formula for inverse variation as follows: $t_1 w_1 = t_2 w_2$. In this case, the t_1 is 10, w_1 is 5, and w_2 is 25 (since you multiply it by 5). So set up the equation as: $10 \times 5 = t_2 \times 25$. $\frac{50}{25} = t_2 = 2$. So what happened to the value of t? It decreased by a factor of 5.

5. **B**   The total must be the sum of the numbers in a ratio, or a multiple of that sum. In this case, 4 + 3 = 7, so the number of socks could be 7 or any multiple of 7. (You can have fractions in a ratio, it's true, but not when you're dealing with socks or people or anything that you can't chop into pieces.)

6. **B**   Here's what to do: Take $\frac{1}{5}$ of 40, which is 8 caramels. Take $\frac{5}{8}$ of 40, which is 25 butterscotches. The caramels and the butterscotches are 8 + 25 = 33. Subtract that from 40 and you've got the fudge.

7. **A** Plug In. Let $x = 2$. If Dixie spent an average of $2 a shirt, then she spent a total of $10 on shirts. Let $y = 4$, and she spent an average of $4 a hat, for a total of $12. Our total is $10 + 12 = 22. Circle that. Now on to the answer choices, plugging in $x = 2$ and $y = 4$. Choice (A) is $5(2) + 3(4) = 22$.

Hard

8. **D** First, multiply the ratio by something big to get rid of the fraction. Any multiple of 6 and 5 will do. So $30\left(\frac{1}{6}\right) : 30\left(\frac{1}{5}\right) = 5:6$. Now you've got $5:6 = 35:x$. Since 35 is 5×7, x is 6×7, or 42. The new ratio is 35:42, which is the same as 5:6.

9. **B** Write down your ratios and label them neatly. You have

$$\frac{b:y}{3:4} \qquad \frac{r:y}{2:3}$$

If the artist uses equal amounts of blue and red, you have to multiply each ratio so that the numbers under b and r are the same:

$$\frac{b:y}{(2)(3:4)} \qquad \frac{r:y}{(2:3)(3)}$$

The result is

$$\frac{b:y}{6:8} \qquad \frac{r:y}{6:9}$$

The yellow is 8 parts + 9 parts = 17 parts, and the total is $6 + 8 + 6 + 9 = 29$ parts. On complicated ratio problems, it's important to organize the information legibly and label everything as you go along, or else you'll find yourself looking at a bunch of meaningless numbers.

10. **B** Plug In the Answers. Start with (B). If the larger radius is 6, the smaller radius is 2 less than that, or 4. The area of the smaller circle is 16π, and the area of the larger circle is 36π. $16\pi:36\pi$ is a ratio of 4:9. (Just divide the whole ratio by 4π.) If you picked (D), you must've had a momentary blackout—that answer is way too appealing to be right on a hard question. If you're going to guess, guess something that is not too good to be true.

A shortcut for averages: If the list of numbers is consecutive, consecutive odd, or consecutive even, then the average will be the middle number. (If the list has an even number of elements, you have to average the two middle numbers.) The average will also be the middle number (or average of the two middle numbers) of any list that goes up in consistent increments. For example, the average of 6, 15, 24, 33, and 42 is 24, since the numbers go up in increments of 9.

PROBLEM SET 8: CHARTS AND DATA

Easy

	Original Price	Sale Price
Store *A*	$25	$20
Store *B*	$20	$15
Store *C*	$30	$25
Store *D*	$35	$30

The chart above shows the original and sale prices of a certain item at each of four different stores. Which of the following stores provides a discount of 20% or more on this item?

    I. Store A

    II. Store B

    III. Store C

A) I only

B) III only

C) I and II only

D) I and III only

Which of the following is most likely the slope of the line of best fit for the scatterplot above?

A) −10

B) −1

C) 1

D) 10

Questions 3 and 4 refer to the following information.

Favorite Ice Cream Flavors

	Men	Women	Total
Chocolate	74	63	137
Vanilla	68	22	90
Strawberry	17	39	56
Cookie Dough	51	87	138
Mint Chip	65	14	79
Total	275	225	500

The table above shows the results of a random survey of 500 men and women. Each individual chose a flavor of ice cream that was his or her favorite.

3

Approximately what percent of the men chose mint chip as their favorite ice cream flavor?

A) 25%

B) 50%

C) 65%

D) 80%

4

If a woman is chosen at random, what is the probability that her favorite ice cream flavor is strawberry?

A) 0.06

B) 0.09

C) 0.11

D) 0.17

Medium

5

Bacteria Reproduction

Time (in seconds) t	Population (in thousands) p
1	2
2	6
3	18
4	54

The table above shows the population growth of a certain bacteria over four seconds. Which one of the following equations shows the relationship between t and p, according to the table?

A) $p = 3t$

B) $p = 2t^2$

C) $p = 2 \times 3t$

D) $p = 2 \times 3^{(t-1)}$

Questions 6-8 refer to the following information.

A coffee distributor randomly polled 200 employees from each of two companies and asked each employee how many cups of coffee he or she drinks per day. The data is shown in the table below.

Employee Coffee Survey

Number of Cups of Coffee	0	1	2	3	4
Company X	5	25	30	40	100
Company Y	20	25	35	45	75

There are 4,000 employees at Company X and 3,000 employees at Company Y.

6

Of the employees polled at Company X, approximately what is the average number of cups of coffee consumed per employee on a given day?

A) 1

B) 2

C) 3

D) 4

7

Based on the poll, the number of employees at Company Y who drank 0 cups of coffee was what percent greater than the number of employees at Company X who drank 0 cups of coffee?

A) 75%

B) 100%

C) 300%

D) 400%

8

What is the difference between the expected total number of employees who drink 1 cup of coffee at Company X and the expected total number of employees who drink 1 cup of coffee at Company Y?

A) 0

B) 25

C) 125

D) 1,000

Hard

Questions 9 and 10 refer to the following information.

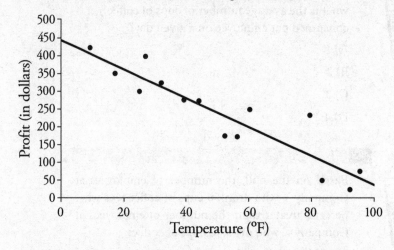

9

The scatterplot above shows the daily profit made by a school store from selling sweatshirts and the average daily temperature for several days in the year 2004. The line of best fit is also shown and has equation $y = -4.1x + 446$. Which of the following best explains how the number -4.1 in the equation relates to the scatterplot?

A) For every 1° increase in average daily temperature, the school store's profit fell by approximately $4.10.

B) For every 1° increase in average daily temperature, the school store's profit increased by approximately $4.10.

C) For every 4.1° increase in average daily temperature, the school store's profit fell by approximately $1.00.

D) For every 4.1° increase in average daily temperature, the school store's profit increased by approximately $1.00.

10

In a given school week, the average daily temperature is 20°F on Monday, Tuesday, and Wednesday and 30°F on Thursday and Friday. Based on the line of best fit, what was the school store's approximate profit during this school week?

A) $325

B) $650

C) $1,475

D) $1,700

ANSWERS AND EXPLANATIONS: PROBLEM SET 8

Easy

1. **C**   Remember that the formula for percent change is $\dfrac{\text{difference}}{\text{original}} \times 100$. The discount at Store A is $\dfrac{5}{25} \times 100 = 20\%$, and the discount at Store B is $\dfrac{5}{20} \times 100 = 25\%$. On the other hand, the discount at Store C is $\dfrac{5}{30} \times 100 = 16.67\%$. Thus, only Stores A and B have discounts of 20% or greater.

2. **B**   Draw a line that connects most of the points. It is a straight line that goes down from left to right, which means it has a negative slope. Only (A) and (B) are negative slopes. Eyeball the line to see that it is not very steep. So, the slope is closer to 1 than 10. Alternatively, you could find points and ballpark the slope. The line roughly includes (50, 50), so the rise and run are the same. Therefore, the slope is –1.

3. **A**   Percent is defined as $\dfrac{\text{part}}{\text{whole}} \times 100$. On the chart, the number of men who chose mint chip is 65, so that's the *part*. The *whole* is the total number of men, which is 275. So the percent is $\dfrac{65}{275} \times 100 = 23.6\%$. This is approximately 25%, so the answer is (A). Once you get the numbers, you can also estimate. Definitely less than half the men chose mint chip, so only (A) would work.

4. **D**   Probability is defined as $\dfrac{\text{what you want}}{\text{total}}$, and in this case, you want the number of women who prefer strawberry out of the number of all the women polled. So the probability is $\dfrac{39}{225}$. Some questions will stop there and leave the probability as a fraction, but the answers here are decimals. Divide 39 by 225 to get about 0.17, which is (D).

Medium

5. **D**   Don't try to figure this one out by deriving an equation. Plug In by testing the numbers in the table against the functions in the answer choices. Plug in $t = 1$ and $p = 2$. Choice (A) is $2 = 3(1)$. This is incorrect, so eliminate (A). Choice (B) is $2 = 2(1)^2$. This is correct, so keep (B). Choice (C) is $2 = 2 \times 3^1$. This is incorrect, so eliminate (C). Choice (D) is $2 = 2 \times 3^{(1-1)}$. This is correct, so keep (D). Now plug $t = 2$ and $p = 6$ into the remaining choices. Choice (B) is $6 = 2(2)^2$. This is incorrect, so eliminate (B). Choice (D) is $6 = 2 \times 3^{(2-1)}$. This is correct and is the only remaining choice, so the answer is (D).

6. **C**   Average is defined as $\dfrac{\text{total}}{\text{\# of things}}$. There are 200 employees at Company X, so that's the number of things. The total is a bit harder to get from the chart. You need to find all the cups of coffee consumed by these 200 employees. Some people drank 0 cups, so you don't need to worry about that. The chart says that 25 people drank 1 cup each, for 25 cups, and 30 people drank 2 cups each, for 60 more cups. There were 40 employees who drank 3 cups each, adding 120 cups, and 100 people drank 4 cups each, adding 400 more cups to the total. Add up all the cups to get $25 + 60 + 120 + 400 = 605$ total cups of coffee. Plug the numbers into the average formula to get $\dfrac{605}{200} = 3.025$. This is approximately 3, so the answer is (C).

7. **C**   Percent change is defined as $\dfrac{\text{difference}}{\text{original}} \times 100$. The chart says that 5 employees at Company X and 20 employees at Company Y drank 0 cups of coffee. The difference is $20 - 5 = 15$. The original is the number of employees from Company X who drank 0 cups. You can tell this because it asks for the "percent greater than," which means that the original must be the smaller one. Therefore, the percent increase is $\dfrac{15}{5} \times 100 = 300\%$, which is (C).

8. **C**   In order to extrapolate poll results to a larger population, find the percent that fit the requirement in the poll and apply it to the general population. In this case, both companies had 25 employees out of the 200 polled that drank 1 cup of coffee. Therefore, $\frac{25}{200} \times 100 = 12.5\%$ of the employees at both companies can be expected to drink one cup of coffee per day. At Company X, there are 4,000 employees, and 12.5% of 4,000 = 500. At Company Y, there are 3,000 employees, and 12.5% of 3,000 = 375. The difference is 500 − 375 = 125, which is (C).

Hard

9. **A**   On tricky questions, look for opportunities to use POE. As the temperature increases, the profits of the store decrease. Look for any answer choices that say otherwise and eliminate them. Both (B) and (D) say that profits will increase with an increase in temperature, so those are incorrect. Test out the remaining answer choices by plugging in some numbers into the equation for the line of best fit. Since this is in the No Calculator section, pick easy numbers. Start with (A) and plug in $x = 0$ and $x = 1$. At $x = 0$, $y = -4.1(0) + 446 = 446$, and at $x = 1$, $y = -4.1(1) + 446 = 441.9$. The difference between these values is $446 - 441.9 = 4.1$, so (A) is true. There is no need to check out (C): (A) is the correct answer.

10. **D**   You could take these values and plug them into the formula to get an exact, but that's a lot of work, especially without the use of a calculator. Instead, use the line of best fit to estimate the profit at these temperatures. Since the answers are spread apart and you are only asked for the "approximate profit," this will get you close enough. When the temperature is 20°F, the line of best fit predicts a profit of about $360. Use your scantron sheet as a straightedge if you have a hard time reading the graph. There are three days in the week with a temperature of 20°, so the profit for those three days is approximately $360 × 3 = $1,080. For the two days with a temperature of 30°, the profit is about $325, so the store earns $325 × 2 = $650 in those two days. In total, the store earns about $1,080 + $650 = $1,730 for the week. This is closest to (D), so that's the answer.

PROBLEM SET 9: EXPONENTS, ROOTS, AND EQUATIONS

Easy

1

If $t^3 = -8$, what is the value of t^2 ?

A) −4

B) −2

C) 2

D) 4

2

If $60 = (7 + 8)(x - 2)$, what is the value of x ?

A) 10

B) 9

C) 7

D) 6

3

If $4x - 2y = 10$ and $7x + 2y = 23$, what is the value of x ?

A) $\dfrac{1}{3}$

B) 1

C) 3

D) 13

Medium

4

Which of the following equations is equal to
$6y + 6x = 6$?

A) $33 = x + y$

B) $11 - x = y$

C) $11 - 2x = y$

D) $4y - 4x = 44$

5

For their science homework, Brenda and Dylan calculated the volume of air that filled a spherical basketball. If the diameter of the basketball was 6, what was the volume of the air inside the basketball, to the nearest integer?

A) 44

B) 100

C) 113

D) 226

6

Which of the following is equivalent to $\dfrac{\sqrt{a} \times \sqrt{b}}{3\sqrt{a} - 2\sqrt{a}}$?

A) $\dfrac{\sqrt{b}}{\sqrt{a}}$

B) $\sqrt{b}$

C) $\dfrac{2\sqrt{a}}{b}$

D) $\sqrt{ab}$

7

On a certain test, Radeesh earned 2 points for every correct answer and lost 1 point for every incorrect answer. If he answered all 30 questions on the test and received a score of 51, how many questions did Radeesh answer incorrectly?

A) 3

B) 7

C) 15

D) 21

Hard

8

If $\frac{1}{2}(z-4)(z+4) = m$, then, in term of z, what is the value of $z^2 - 16$?

A) $\sqrt{m}$

B) $\frac{m}{2}$

C) m

D) $2m$

9

If $(y+5)^2 = 49$, then which one of the following could be the value of $(y+3)^2$?

A)   1

B)   64

C)   81

D) 225

10

If $a - b = 4$, $b - 6 = c$, $c - 2 = d$, and $a + d = 4$, what is the value of a?

A)   4

B)   8

C) 16

D) It cannot be determined from the information given.

ANSWERS AND EXPLANATIONS: PROBLEM SET 9

Easy

1.   **D**   Take the cube root of both sides to get $t = -2$, and $t^2 = (-2)^2 = 4$.

2.   **D**   Plug In the Answers. Try (B) first: $(15)(9 - 2) = (15)(7) = 105$. It should equal 60, so you need a much smaller number. Try (D): $(15)(6 - 2) = (15)(4) = 60$. It works. Or you could solve the equation algebraically:

$$60 = 15(x - 2)$$
$$60 = 15x - 30$$
$$90 = 15x$$
$$6 = x$$

3. **C** Stack 'em and add:

$$
\begin{aligned}
4x - 2y &= 10 \\
\underline{7x + 2y} &= \underline{23} \\
11x &= 33 \\
x &= 3
\end{aligned}
$$

Medium

4. **B** Try reducing the equation in the question first, by dividing the whole thing by 6. That leaves you with $x + y = 11$. That's the same as (B), if you just move the x to the other side.

5. **C** Don't worry—you weren't supposed to know this formula. It's provided at the start of each math section, so don't get freaked out. Just use the information in the question to solve for V, using your calculator. If the diameter of the basketball was 6, the radius was 3:

$$
V = \frac{4}{3}\pi r^3, \text{ so } V = \frac{4}{3}\pi(3^3) = \frac{4}{3}\pi(27) = 36\pi = 113
$$

You may see some totally unfamiliar formula on the test—physics, for instance—but you don't have to understand the formula or know anything about it. All you have to do is substitute in any value they give you and solve for the variable they ask for.

6. **B** Remember that you can multiply or divide what's under a square root sign and add or subtract when what's under the square root sign is the same. Begin by simplifying the denominator.

$$
\frac{\sqrt{a} \cdot \sqrt{b}}{3\sqrt{a} - 2\sqrt{a}} = \frac{\sqrt{a} \cdot \sqrt{b}}{\sqrt{a}} = \sqrt{b}.
$$

7. **A** Plug In the Answers. If Radeesh got 2 points for every right answer, and the test had 30 questions, the top score was 60. If he got a 51, he did pretty well, so start with (A). (Remember, the answer choices represent the number of questions he answered incorrectly.) If he missed 3, then he got 27 right. $27 \times 2 = 54$. Subtract 3 for 3 wrong answers, and you get 51.

[Don't worry if you didn't see which answer to start with. If you started with (C), it gave you way too many wrong answers, didn't it? So cross off (C) and (D) and you've only got two left to try.]

Hard

8. **D** The easiest way to solve this question is to recognize that $(z - 4)$ $(z + 4) = (z - 16)^2$. Thus, you can rewrite the initial equation as $\frac{1}{2}$ $(z - 16)^2 = m$. Thus, $z - 16^2 = 2m$. Otherwise, Plug In. Try $z = 6$, which means $m = 10$. The value of $z^2 - 16$ is 20, which is twice as much as m, or $2m$.

9. **C** Since $(y + 5)^2 = 49$, take the square root of both sides. Don't forget that the result could be positive or negative, so $y + 5 = \pm 7$. Consider both cases. If $y + 5 = 7$, then $y = 2$. In this case, $(y + 3)^2 = (2 + 3)^2 = 5^2 = 25$. This is not a choice, so consider the other case. If $y + 5 = -7$, then $y = -12$. In this case, $(y + 3)^2 = (-12 + 3)^2 = (-9)^2 = 81$, which is (C).

10. **B** Start off by eliminating (D), as that would be too easy for a complicated looking question toward the end. Before you start the lengthy process of substitution, try stack-and-add. You need to bring all of the variables to the left and all of the numbers to the right, so your stack will look like this:

$$a - b = 4$$
$$b - c = 6$$
$$c - d = 2$$
$$a + d = 4$$

Add everything up. It turns out that b, c, and d disappear, leaving $2a = 16$, or $a = 8$.

PROBLEM SET 10: LINES, ANGLES, AND COORDINATES

Easy

1

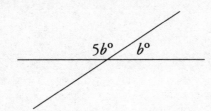

In the figure above, what is the value of $3a - a$?

A) 55°

B) 90°

C) 110°

D) 165°

2

In the figure above, what is the value of b ?

A) 20°

B) 30°

C) 40°

D) 45°

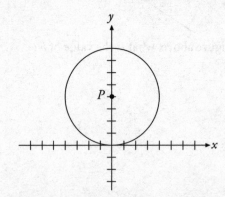

In the *xy*-plane above, what is the value of the *x*-coordinate of Point *A* minus the *y*-coordinate of Point *B* ?

A) –2

B) –1

C) 3

D) 5

Medium

4

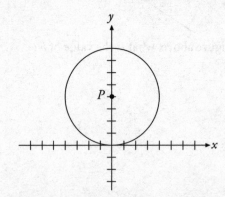

Point *P* is the center of the cirlce shown above, which has a radius of 4. Which of the following points lies on circle *P* ?

A) (4, 0)

B) (0, 4)

C) (–4, 4)

D) (4, 3)

5

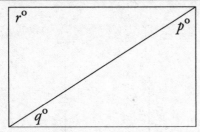

In the rectangle above, what is the value of $p + q - r$?

A) 0°

B) 15°

C) 35°

D) 50°

6

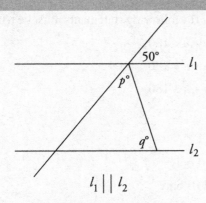

$l_1 \mid\mid l_2$

Note: Figure not drawn to scale.

In the figure above, what is the value of $p + q$?

A) 150°

B) 130°

C) 90°

D) 70°

7

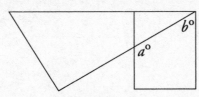

The figure above is formed by a triangle overlapping a rectangle. What is the value of $a + b$?

A) 90°

B) 150°

C) 180°

D) 270°

Hard

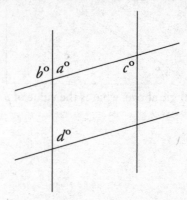

Note: Figure not drawn to scale.

Which of the following statements must be true?

  I. $a + b < 180$

 II. $a + d = 180$

III. $a + d > 180$

A) None

B) II only

C) I and II only

D) II and III only

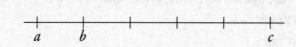

The tick marks on the number line above are equally spaced. If 2 is halfway between b and c, and the value of $c - a$ is 10, what is the value of b ?

A) −4

B) −2

C) 0

D) 6

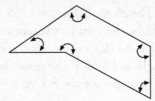

What is the total number of degrees of the marked angles?

A) 180

B) 360

C) 540

D) 720

ANSWERS AND EXPLANATIONS: PROBLEM SET 10

Easy

1. **C** A triangle has 180°. So $90 + 35 + a = 180$, and $a = 55$. Plug that into the equation and get $3(55) - 55 = 110$.

2. **B** $5b$ and b lie on a straight line, so $5b + b = 180$ and $b = 30$.

3. **D** The x-coordinate of Point A is 3, and the y-coordinate of Point B is -2. So $3 - (-2) = 5$.

Medium

4. **C** The coordinates are given, so don't worry about trying to make an equation or manipulating the radius or anything like that. Just plot the points and see which one falls on the circle. Remember that on the circle means on the circumference rather than inside the circumference. Choices (A), (B), and (D) are all inside the circle. Only (C) is on the circumference.

5. **A** As always, mark whatever info you can on your diagram: $r = 90$, and the angle on the bottom right is also 90, because this is a rectangle. $p + q = 90$, because they are the two remaining angles in a right triangle. That means $p + q - r = 90 - 90 = 0$.

6. **B** Again, mark info on the diagram. The unmarked angle of the triangle is 50° because l_1 and l_2 are parallel, and the unmarked angle and the 50° angle are both small, so $50 + p + q = 180$ and $p + q = 130°$. (You can't figure out what p and q are individually, but the question doesn't ask you to anyway.)

7. **C**   Estimate first. The angle marked *a* is greater than 90, and you are adding *b* to it. Therefore, (A) is too small. Choice (D) looks too big, since that would be the sum of two obtuse angles, and *b* is less than 90. Now only (B) and (C) are left. To figure out the sum of the angles, ignore the triangle and look at the quadrilateral in the bottom half of the rectangle. The angles are $a + b + 90 + 90$. Since a quadrilateral has 360°, $a + b = 180$.

Hard

8. **A**   It's important to realize what you *don't* know: Are any of these lines parallel? *You don't know.* So you can't draw any conclusions at all other than the rule that a line contains 180°. Keep this simple and imagine that all the intersecting lines are perpendicular. In this case, $a + b = 180$, so I is false. Also, $a + d = 180$, so II is true but III is false. Eliminate any choice that includes I or III: Choices (C) and (D) are out. Because the lines do not have to be parallel, there is no necessary relationship between *a* and *d*. It could be the case that *a* is a right angle and *d* is acute. For example, *a* could be 90 and *d* could be 60. In this case, $a + d = 150$, so II is false. Eliminate (B). Only (A) remains.

9. **B**   The best way to approach this question is to Plug In the Answers. Try (B) and suppose *b* is –2. Because the midpoint between *b* and *c* is 2, you can see that each tick mark represents a value of 2 more than the previous tick mark. Thus, *a* is –4 and *c* is 6. Now, you have to check this against the remaining information in the question. So $c - a$ must be 10. Is it? Yes, so (B) is our answer!

10. **C**   Estimate first and see what you can cross out. Since you have two angles that are bigger than 90 and one angle that's bigger than 180, you should be able at least to cross out (A) and (B). To figure out the exact number of degrees, divide the figure into three triangles:

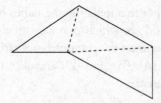

The total degrees will be $180 \times 3 = 540$. Alternatively, know that each side added to a figure adds 180°. A three-sided figure (i.e., a triangle) has 180°, so a four-sided figure has 360°, and a five-sided figure has 540°.

PROBLEM SET 11: TRIANGLES

Easy

1

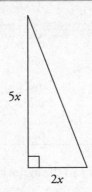

If the area of the triangle above is 6, what is its perimeter?

A) 11

B) 12

D) 15

D) 16

2

If $x = 3$, what is the area of the triangle above?

A) 10

B) 21

C) 30

D) 45

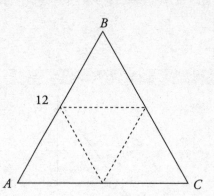

If equilateral triangle *ABC* is cut by three lines, as shown, to form four equilateral triangles of equal area, what is the length of a side of one of the smaller triangles?

A) 3

B) 4

C) 5

D) 6

Medium

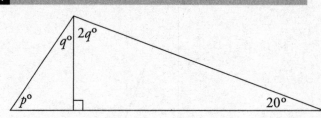

What is the value of *p* in the figure above?

A) 50

B) 55

C) 60

D) 70

A movie theater is 3 blocks due north of a supermarket, and a beauty parlor is 4 blocks due east of the movie theater. How many blocks long is the street that runs directly from the supermarket to the beauty parlor?

A) 2.5

B) 3

C) 5

D) 7

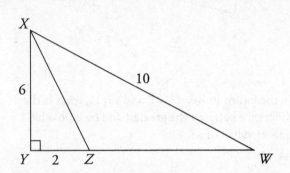

What is the area of triangle *WXZ* in the figure above?

A) 6

B) 12

C) 18

D) 24

Hard

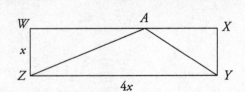

In the figure above, what is the area of triangle *YAZ*?

A) $3x$

B) $5x$

C) $2x^2$

D) $4x^2$

8

A square is inscribed in a circle with area 9π. What is the area of the square?

A) $3\sqrt{2}$

B) $9\sqrt{2}$

C) 18

D) 36

9

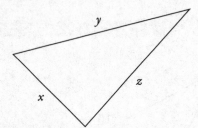

In the figure above, if $x = 7$ and $y = 11$, what is the difference between the greatest and least possible integer values of z ?

A) 11

B) 12

C) 13

D) 14

10

An equilateral triangle with a perimeter of 12 is inscribed in a circle. What is the area of the circle?

A) $\dfrac{16\pi}{9}$

B) $\dfrac{4\pi\sqrt{3}}{3}$

C) 3π

D) $\dfrac{16\pi}{3}$

ANSWERS AND EXPLANATIONS: PROBLEM SET 11

Easy

1. **B**   There are several ways to get this question: You could recognize that it's a Pythagorean triple (3:4:5), which would give you the length of the unmarked leg. Or you could set up the following equation:

$$a = \frac{1}{2}bh$$

$\frac{1}{2}b(4) = 6$ so $2b = 6$ and $b = 3$. All that did was substitute the height and the area, both of which are given in the problem, into the formula for the area of a triangle. Either way, the perimeter is the sum of the sides, which is $3 + 4 + 5 = 12$.

2. **D**   If $x = 3$, then the base of the triangle is 6 and the height is 15. That would mean the area is $\frac{1}{2}(6)(15) = 45$.

3. **D**   Because all the small triangles and the big triangle are equilateral, each vertex of the small triangles bisects a side of the big triangle, which means that each side is 6. (Don't forget to estimate.)

Medium

4. **B**   Start with the triangle to the right of the height line. As the height forms an angle of 90 and the given angle is 20, the third angle is 70 (180 – 110). Thus, $2q = 70$, and $q = 35$. Now go to the triangle to the left of the height line. As the height forms an angle of 90 and q is 35, p is 55.

5. **C**   Draw a little map, which should look like this:

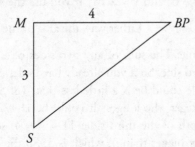

Now you have a 3:4:5 right triangle, so the street from the supermarket to the beauty parlor is 5 blocks long.

6. **C** Use the Pythagorean Theorem to find the base of triangle WYZ: $6^2 + b^2 = 10^2$. The base is 8. (This is the 6-8-10 triple, so you didn't really need to use the Pythagorean Theorem.) As $YZ = 2$, the base of triangle WXZ is 6. Even though segment XY lies outside triangle WXZ, segment XY is still perpendicular to an extension of the base, thus representing the height. Since its length is 6, the height of the triangle is 6. Thus, the area ($\frac{1}{2}bh$) is 18.

Hard

7. **C** Plug In. If $x = 2$, then ZY is 8 and WZ is 2. (Write that on your diagram.) To get the area of YAZ, notice that WZ is the height of the triangle, so $\frac{1}{2}(8)(2) = 8$. Plug 2 back into the answers. Choice (A) is $3(2) = 6$, so eliminate (A). Choice (B) is $5(2) = 10$, so eliminate (B). Choice (C) is $2(2^2) = 8$, so keep (C). Choice (D) is $4(2^2) = 16$, so eliminate (D). The answer is (C).

8. **C** As there is no diagram, first draw a square in a circle. As the area of the circle is 9π, the radius is 3 (Area = πr^2). How does this help? Often on the SAT, questions involving squares are really about the diagonal of the square, so draw in the diagonal. The diagonal is the diameter of the circle, so the diagonal is 6. You can use the Pythagorean Theorem or your knowledge of 45-45-90 triangles to figure out the sides. Label the sides of the square x. If you use the Pythagorean Theorem, you will solve $x^2 + x^2 = 6^2$ and $x = \sqrt{18}$. If you use the 45-45-90 relationships, you will get $x = \frac{6}{\sqrt{2}}$. Either way, the area of the square is 18.

9. **B** Here's the rule: The sum of any two sides of a triangle must be more than the third side. So if you already have sides of 7 and 11, the longest the third side could be is a little less than 18. Since the third side has to be an integer, the longest it could be is 17. Now for the shortest possible length of the third side: $11 - 7 = 4$, so the third side has to be an integer bigger than 4, which is 5. So the difference between the greatest possible and the least possible is $17 - 5 = 12$.

10. **D**   There is no figure provided, so draw your own.

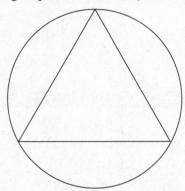

The perimeter of the equilateral triangle is 12, so each side is 12 ÷ 3 = 4. The question asks for the area of the circle, so find a radius. A radius can be drawn from each vertex of the triangle to the center of the circle. Each radius bisects the angle in each corner of the triangle. Since all the angles in an equilateral triangle are 60°, each newly formed angle is 30°. Take one of the new triangles, say the one on the bottom. Because it has two 30° angles, the third angle must be 180° – 30° – 30° = 120°. Because two sides of this triangle are radii, it is isosceles and thus has a perpendicular bisector. Drawing the perpendicular bisector of the base breaks this triangle into two 30-60-90 triangles, like below.

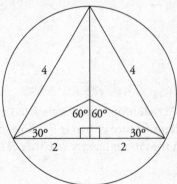

In a 30-60-90 right triangle, the side opposite the 30° is x, the side opposite the 60° angle is $x\sqrt{3}$, and the side opposite the 90° angle is $2x$.

Since the side opposite the 60° angle is 2, $x\sqrt{3} = 2$. Thus, $x = \dfrac{2}{\sqrt{3}}$ and $2x = \dfrac{4}{\sqrt{3}}$. Because the radius is the side opposite the 90°, the radius is $\dfrac{4}{\sqrt{3}}$. Thus, the area of the circle is $A = \pi r^2 = \pi \left(\dfrac{4}{\sqrt{3}} \right)^2 = \dfrac{16\pi}{3}$.

PROBLEM SET 12: CIRCLES, QUADRILATERALS, AND VOLUME

Easy

1

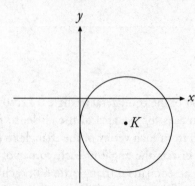

Point *K* is the center of the circle above, and the coordinates of Point *K* are (2, –1). What is the area of the circle?

A) π

B) 2π

C) 4π

D) 8π

2

Circle *P* has a radius of 7, and Circle *R* has a diameter of 8. The circumference of Circle *P* is how much greater than the circumference of Circle *R* ?

A)   π

B)   6π

C) 16π

D) 33π

3

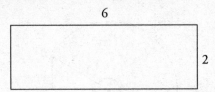

6

2

How many squares with sides of 1 could fit into the rectangle above?

A) 3

B) 4

C) 6

D) 12

Medium

4

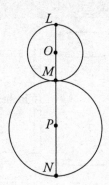

In the figure above, LM is $\frac{1}{3}$ of LN. If the radius of the circle with center P is 6, what is the area of the circle with center O ?

A) 4π

B) 9π

C) 12π

D) 18π

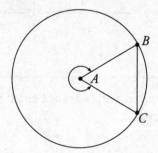

In the figure above, the circle has center A, and $BC = AB$. What is the degree measure of the marked angle?

A) 60°

B) 270°

C) 300°

D) 340°

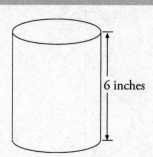

6 inches

In the figure above, the radius of the base of the cylinder is half its height. What is the approximate volume of the cylinder in cubic inches?

A) 28

B) 57

C) 117

D) 170

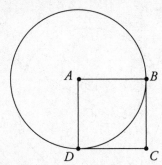

7

Points *D* and *B* lie on the circle above with center *A*. If square *ABCD* has an area of 16, what is the length of arc *BD* ?

A) 2π

B) 4

C) 8

D) 4π

Hard

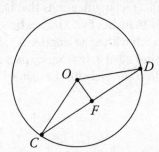

In the figure above, what is the circumference of the circle with center *O*, if *COD* is 120° and *OF* bisects *CD* and has a length of 1.5 ?

A) $\dfrac{2\pi}{3}$

B) $\dfrac{3\pi}{2}$

C) 6π

D) 9π

9

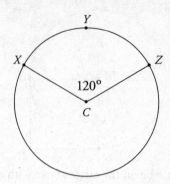

In the figure above, C is the center of a circle. If the length of the arc XYZ is 4π, what is the radius of the circle?

A)   4

B) $2\sqrt{3}$

C)   6

D)   12

10

Jeremy will fill a rectangular crate that has inside dimensions of 18 inches by 15 inches by 9 inches with cubical tiles, each with edge lengths of 3. If the tiles are packaged in sets of 8, how many packages will Jeremy need to completely fill the crate?

A)   11

B)   12

C)   90

D) 101

ANSWERS AND EXPLANATIONS: PROBLEM SET 12

Easy

1. **C**   Because the circle is tangent to the y-axis, the radius that intersects the y-axis is perpendicular to the y-axis, and thus parallel to the x-axis. Since the radius is parallel to the x-axis, the y-coordinate is constant. To find the length of the radius, find the difference between the x-coordinates of the end points. On the y-axis, the x-coordinate is 0. Since the center at K has an x-coordinate of 2, the length of the radius is $2 - 0 = 2$. Then use the formula for area of a circle: $\pi r^2 = \pi(2^2) = 4\pi$.

2. **B** Circumference can be found with either the formula $2\pi r$ or πd. You have the radius of one circle and the diameter of the other, so use both. The circumference of Circle P is $2\pi r = 2\pi(7) = 14\pi$. The circumference of Circle R is $\pi d = 8\pi$. Now just subtract. If you picked (D), you calculated area instead of circumference.

3. **D** Drawing on the diagram could help. How many sides of 1 can fit along the long edge of the rectangle? 6. And how many rows will fit along the short edge? 2. Now just multiply $6 \times 2 = 12$. Or draw them in and count them up.

Medium

4. **B** Write in 6 by the radius of the bigger circle. That makes the diameter of the bigger circle 12. If LM (the diameter of the smaller circle) is $\frac{1}{3}$ the length of LN, the equation is $\left(\frac{1}{3}\right)(12 + x) = x$. $4 = x - \frac{x}{3}$, and $x = 6$. (You don't have to write an equation. You could estimate and try some numbers. Doesn't LM look like it's about half of MN? It is.) If the diameter of the smaller circle is 6, then its radius is 3 and its area is 9π.

5. **C** Estimate first. The marked angle is way more than 180—in fact, it's not that far from 360. Cross out (A). You know $AC = AB$ because they're both radii. That means $BC = AB = AC$, and the triangle is equilateral. So angle BAC is 60°. Subtract that from 360 and you're in business. (Even if all you could do was estimate, go ahead and take a guess.)

6. **D** If the radius is half the height, then the radius is 3. To get the volume of a cylinder, multiply the area of the base times the height—in this case, $\pi(3^2) \times 6 = 54\pi$, which is approximately 170.

7. **A** If the square has an area of 16, then the side of the square is 4. Write that on your diagram. Now you know the radius of the circle is also 4, so the circumference is 8π. Angle BAD has 90°, since it's a corner of the square. And since 90 is $\frac{1}{4}$ of 360, arc BD is $\frac{1}{4}$ of the circumference. So arc BD is $\left(\frac{1}{4}\right)(8\pi)$, or 2π. If you estimated first, you could have crossed out (D), and maybe even (C).

Hard

8. **C**   Write the info on your diagram. If *OF* bisects *CD*, it also bisects angle *COD*, making two 60° angles. Now there are two 30-60-90 triangles. If the shortest leg of one of those triangles is 1.5, then the hypotenuse is 2 × 1.5, or 3. Aha! That distance is also the radius of the circle, so the circumference is 6π.

9. **C**   The ratio of the length of an arc to the circumference of the circle is the same as the ratio of the degree measure of the arc to the 360 degrees of the circle. As 120° is one-third of the circle, the length of the arc is one-third of the circumference. Thus, the circumference of the circle is 12π. As Circumference = 2π*r*, the radius is 6.

10. **B**   To find the number of tiles that will fit in the crate, you must divide the dimensions of the crate by all three dimensions of the tiles:

$$\frac{18 \times 15 \times 9}{3 \times 3 \times 3} = 90$$

But don't select 90 as your answer! The question asks how many packages of 8 tiles are needed. So, divide 90 by 8, which equals 11 plus a remainder. As 11 packages will contain only 88 of the 90 tiles needed, Jeremy must buy a 12th package.

> One more thing: Circle questions tend to appear most often in the later medium and hard questions.

PROBLEM SET 13: ADVANCED GEOMETRY

Easy

1

The density of an object is equal to the mass of the object divided by the volume of the object. What is the volume, in square feet, of an object with a mass of 2,000 pounds and a density of 500 pounds per square foot?

A) 1,000,000

B)   1,500

C)   4

D)   0.25

2

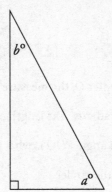

In the triangle above, if $\cos a = \dfrac{5}{13}$, what is $\sin b$?

A) $\dfrac{5}{13}$

B) $\dfrac{5}{12}$

C) $\dfrac{12}{13}$

D) $\dfrac{12}{5}$

3

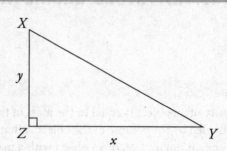

Given the right triangle above, which of the following is equivalent to $\frac{y}{x}$?

A) tan X

B) tan Y

C) cos X

D) cos Y

Medium

4

In a circle with center O, the measure of central angle POQ is $\frac{3\pi}{2}$ radians. The length of the arc formed by central angle POQ is what fraction of the circumference of the circle?

A) $\frac{3}{16}$

B) $\frac{3}{8}$

C) $\frac{3}{4}$

D) $\frac{3}{2}$

5

In a right triangle, one angle measures $y°$, where $\cos y = \dfrac{3}{5}$. What is $\sin(90° - y°)$?

A) $\dfrac{3}{5}$

B) $\dfrac{3}{4}$

C) $\dfrac{4}{5}$

D) $\dfrac{4}{3}$

6

In a right triangle, $\sin x° = \cos y°$. If $x = 3c + 14$ and $y = 7c + 11$, what is the value of c ?

A)　3.5

B)　6.5

C)　11.5

D)　22.5

7

In triangle PQR, $\angle Q$ is a right angle, $QR = 24$, and $PR = 26$. Triangle XYZ is similar to triangle PQR, where vertices X, Y, and Z correspond to vertices P, Q, and R, respectively, and each side of triangle XYZ is $\dfrac{1}{2}$ the length of the corresponding side of triangle PQR. What is the value of $\sin Z$?

A) $\dfrac{5}{13}$

B) $\dfrac{5}{12}$

C) $\dfrac{12}{13}$

D) $\dfrac{12}{5}$

Hard

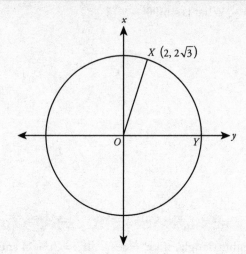

In the *xy*-plane above, the circle has center *O*, and the measure of ∠*XOY* is $\dfrac{\pi}{n}$ radians. What is the value of *n* ?

A) 1

B) 3

C) 6

D) 12

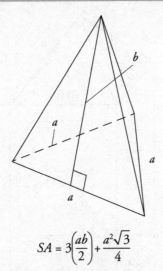

$$SA = 3\left(\frac{ab}{2}\right) + \frac{a^2\sqrt{3}}{4}$$

The formula above can be used to find the surface area of the right pyramid with equilateral triangular base shown, where *a* is the length of each side of the triangular base and *b* is the slant height of the lateral face. What must the expression 1.5*ab* represent?

A) The area of the base

B) The area of a lateral face

C) The area of the base and one lateral face

D) The sum of the areas of the lateral faces

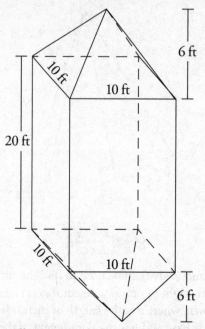

An art installation is built from a rectangular solid and two pyramids with dimensions as indicated by the figure above. Which is the volume of the art installation in square feet?

A) 2,400

B) 2,000

C) 400

D) 200

ANSWERS AND EXPLANATIONS: PROBLEM SET 13

Easy

1. **C** Translate the first sentence into an equation. If *the density of an object is equal to the mass of the object divided by the volume of the object,* then $d = \frac{m}{V}$. Since the density is 500 pounds per square foot and the mass is 2,000 pounds, plug $d = 500$ and $m = 2,000$ into the equation to get $500 = \frac{2,000}{V}$. Multiply both sides by V to get $500V = 2,000$. Divide both sides by 500 to get $V = 4$. The answer is (C).

2. **A**   The question says that $\cos a = \dfrac{5}{13}$, and $\cos = \dfrac{\text{adj}}{\text{hyp}}$, so place 5 adjacent to a and 13 as the hypotenuse. The question asks for $\sin b$, which is $\dfrac{\text{opp}}{\text{hyp}}$. You just labeled the side opposite of b as 5 and you know the hypotenuse is 13, so $\sin b = \dfrac{\text{opp}}{\text{hyp}} = \dfrac{5}{13}$. The answer is (A).

3. **B**   The question asks for which choice is equivalent to $\dfrac{y}{x}$. The answer choices include trig functions, so use SOHCAHTOA. The functions included in the choices are cos, which is equal to $\dfrac{\text{adj}}{\text{hyp}}$, and tan, which is equal to $\dfrac{\text{opp}}{\text{adj}}$. To find cosine, the length of the hypotenuse is needed, but it is not given. Eliminate the two choices that include cosine: (C) and (D). Therefore, the answer will be either tan X or tan Y. Since $\tan = \dfrac{\text{opp}}{\text{adj}}$, determine which angle y is opposite and x is adjacent to. Look at the figure to see that this is Y, which is (B). In the case of tan X, x is opposite the angle and y is adjacent to the angle, so $\dfrac{\text{opp}}{\text{adj}} = \dfrac{x}{y}$. This is not what the question asks for, so eliminate (A). The answer is (B).

Medium

4. **C**   When a question asks about the arc, use the formula $\dfrac{\text{arc}}{\text{circumference}} = \dfrac{\text{central angle}}{2\pi}$ with the measure of the central angle in radians. Since you're literally looking for the fraction of the arc's length to the circumference of the circle, all that is needed to solve this problem is $\dfrac{\text{central angle}}{2\pi}$. Substitute the central angle of $\dfrac{3\pi}{2}$ into the formula to get $\dfrac{\text{central angle}}{2\pi} = \dfrac{\frac{3\pi}{2}}{2\pi}$. To solve $\dfrac{\frac{3\pi}{2}}{2\pi}$, put the denominator over 1 and multiply the numerator by the reciprocal of the denominator

$$\frac{\frac{3\pi}{2}}{\frac{2\pi}{1}} = \frac{3\pi}{2} \times \frac{1}{2\pi} = \frac{3\pi}{4\pi} = \frac{3}{4}.$$ The answer is (C).

5.　**A**　The question asks for $\sin(90° - y°)$. To answer this, use the formula $\cos x = \sin(90° - x°)$. Since $\cos y = \frac{3}{5}$, $\sin(90° - y°) = \frac{3}{5}$. The answer is (A). If you forget the formula, draw a right triangle and label y and the sides you know given $\cos y$. The side that measures 3 will be adjacent to y, and 5 is the hypotenuse.

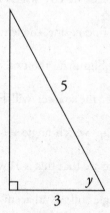

Whatever y is, the top angle will be $90 - y$, since there are 180° in a triangle. Therefore, the sine of the top angle is $\sin(90° - y°) = \frac{3}{5}$.

6.　**B**　The question says that $\sin x = \cos y$. Use the fact that $\sin x = \cos(90 - x)$. Therefore, $y = 90 - x$. The question also says that $x = 3c + 14$ and $y = 7c + 11$. Substitute these into $y = 90 - x$ to get $7c + 11 = 90 - (3c + 14)$. Distribute the negative to get $7c + 11 = 90 - 3c - 14$. Simplify the right side to get $7c + 11 = 76 - 3c$. Add $3c$ to both sides to get $10c + 11 = 76$. Subtract 11 from both sides to get $10c = 65$. Divide both sides by 10 to get $c = 6.5$. The answer is (B). If you forget this rule about the complimentary angles in a right triangle, you can always use PITA. Starting with (B), plug in 6.5 for c. The value of $x = 3(6.5) + 14 = 19.5 + 14 = 33.5$, and the value of $y = 7(6.5) + 11 = 45.5 + 11 = 56.5$. Now, with your calculator in degree mode, see if $\sin(33.5°) = \cos(56.5°)$. It does, so (B) is correct.

7.　**A**　The question asks for the value of $\sin Z$. According to the question, triangles PQR and XYZ are similar. Similar triangles, by definition, have congruent corresponding angles. Since $\angle Z$ corresponds to $\angle R$, $\angle Z \cong \angle R$. Therefore, $\sin Z = \sin R$. Since there is more information directly provided about triangle PQR than about triangle XYZ, use this information to determine $\sin R$, which will be equal to the answer. Start by sketching triangle PQR.

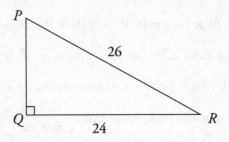

The value of sin R is $\dfrac{\text{opposite}}{\text{hypotenuse}}$. The hypotenuse is 26. Determine the opposite side. There are two ways to do this. One is to use the Pythagorean Theorem. However, since a calculator is not allowed on this question, it may be difficult to do this with large numbers. The other way is to notice that 24:26 = 12:13. Therefore, this is a 5:12:13 right triangle with the sides multiplied by 2. PQ represents the 5 side, so $PQ = 2 \times 5 = 10$. Therefore, the opposite side is 10. Plug this in to get $\cos R = \dfrac{10}{26}$. Reduce the fraction by 2 to get $\cos R = \dfrac{5}{13}$. The answer is (A).

Hard

8. **B**   The question asks about the measure of $\angle XOY$. Notice that point X has a y-coordinate of $2\sqrt{3}$. An instance of $\sqrt{3}$ in a geometry question will often be an indicator of a 30-60-90 right triangle. In the figure, draw a segment from point X that is perpendicular to segment OY to form a right triangle. For reference, we'll call the point of intersection Z.

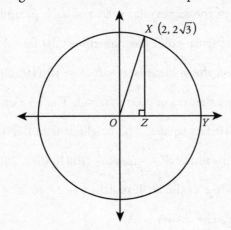

In the figure, $OZ = 2$ and $XZ = 2\sqrt{3}$. In a 30-60-90 right triangle, the sides opposite the 30° angle, the 60° angle, and the 90° angle, respectively, are in a ratio of $1:\sqrt{3}:2$. In this triangle, that ratio is multiplied by 2. Since $\angle XOY$ is opposite segment XZ, which has measure $2\sqrt{3}$, it is a 60° angle. Because the question asks for the measure in radians, convert to radians using the proportion $\dfrac{\text{radians}}{\text{degrees}} = \dfrac{\pi}{180}$. Substitute 60° to get $\dfrac{r}{60} = \dfrac{\pi}{180}$. Cross-multiply to get $180r = 60\pi$. Divide both sides by 180 to get $r = \dfrac{60\pi}{180} = \dfrac{\pi}{3}$. The question says that the measure of $\angle XOY$ is $\dfrac{\pi}{n}$, so $\dfrac{\pi}{n} = \dfrac{\pi}{3}$ and $n = 3$. The answer is (B).

9. **D** The question asks for what $1.5ab$ represents, but $1.5ab$ doesn't actually appear directly in the equation. The expression ab, however, does appear as part of the term $3\left(\dfrac{ab}{2}\right)$. Notice that $3\left(\dfrac{ab}{2}\right) = \dfrac{3ab}{2} = 1.5ab$. Therefore, the question is really asking for what the first term represents. Why would the expression $\dfrac{ab}{2}$ be multiplied by 3? The definition of surface area is the sum of the areas of each face. Since there are 3 lateral faces, determine whether $\dfrac{ab}{2}$ represents the area of each face. The area of a triangle is $A = \dfrac{1}{2}bh$. The base of the lateral side is a and the height is b, so the area is $A = \dfrac{1}{2}bh = \dfrac{ab}{2}$. Since the area of one lateral face is $\dfrac{ab}{2}$, the area of all three must add up to $3\left(\dfrac{ab}{2}\right) = 1.5$. The answer is (D).

10. **A** In order to determine the volume of the art installation, find the volume of the rectangular solid and each pyramid and get the sum. The rectangular solid has dimensions 10 feet, 10 feet, and 20 feet. Therefore, the volume is $V = lwh = (10)(10)(20) = 2{,}000$ ft³. Now determine the area of each pyramid. The base of the pyramid is a 10 feet by 10 feet square. The height is 6 feet. Therefore, the volume of each pyramid is $V = \dfrac{1}{3}lwh = \dfrac{1}{3}(10)(10)(6) = 200$ ft³. Therefore, the total volume of the art installation is 2,000 ft³ + 200 ft³ + 200 ft³ = 2,400 ft³. The answer is (A).

PROBLEM SET 14: FUNCTIONS

Easy

1

If the function f has three distinct zeros, which of the following represents the graph of f in the xy-plane?

A)
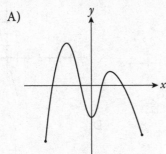

B)
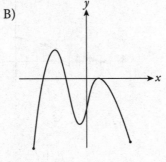

C)
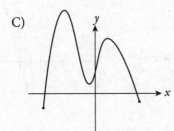

D)
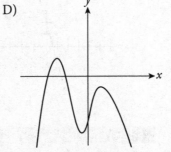

2

In the xy-plane, the graph of the function g has zeroes at -4, 2, and 4. Which of the following could define g?

A) $g(x) = (x - 4)(x - 2)(x + 4)$

B) $g(x) = (x - 4)^2(x - 2)$

C) $g(x) = (x - 4)(x + 2)(x + 4)$

D) $g(x) = (x + 2)(x + 4)^2$

3

If $f(x) = 2x + 1$ and $f(a) = 2$, what is the value of a?

A) $-\dfrac{1}{2}$

B) $\dfrac{1}{2}$

C) 2

D) 5

Medium

If $f(x) = 4x + 2$, which of the following is the graph of $f(x)$?

A)

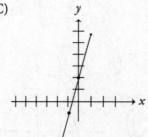

B)

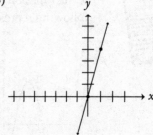

C)

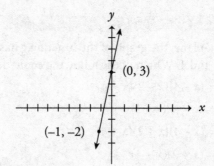

D)

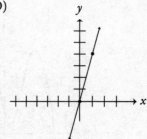

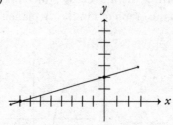

(0, 3)

(−1, −2)

If the graph above is that of $f(x)$, which of the following could be $f(x)$?

A) $f(x) = \dfrac{1}{5}x + \dfrac{1}{3}$

B) $f(x) = \dfrac{1}{5}x + 3$

C) $f(x) = 3x + 5$

D) $f(x) = 5x + 3$

6

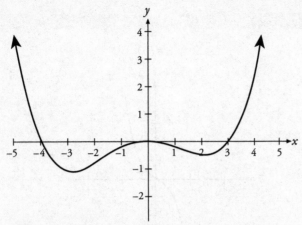

Which of the following could be the equation of the graph in the xy-plane shown above?

A) $f(x) = x(x + 3)(x - 4)$

B) $f(x) = x(x + 4)(x - 3)$

C) $f(x) = x^2(x + 3)(x - 4)$

D) $f(x) = x^2(x + 4)(x - 3)$

7

If $f(x) = 2x^2 + 8x + 2$, for what values of x does $f(x) = 0$?

A) $x = -8 \pm 4\sqrt{3}$

B) $x = -8 \pm \sqrt{3}$

C) $x = -2 \pm \sqrt{3}$

D) $x = -8 \pm \dfrac{\sqrt{40}}{2}$

8

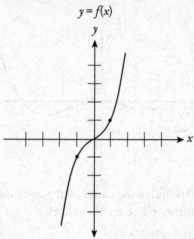

$$y = f(x)$$

If the graph above shows the function $f(x) = x^3$, which one of the following graphs shows $f(x) = (x + 2)^3 - 3$?

A)

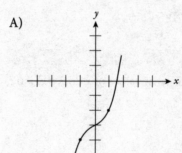

B)

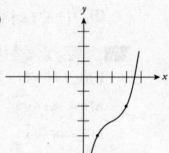

C)

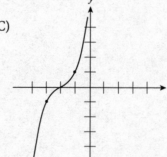

D)

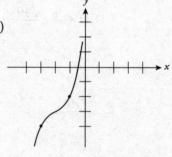

9

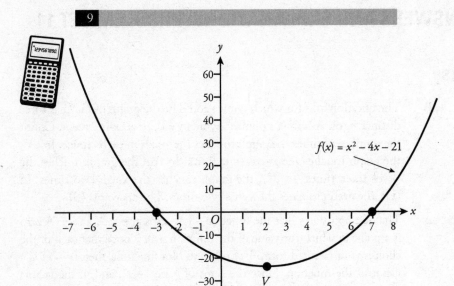

$f(x) = x^2 - 4x - 21$

Which of the following is an equivalent form of the equation of the function graphed above from which the coordinates of the vertex V can be identified as constants in the equation?

A) $f(x) = (x - 3)(x + 7)$

B) $f(x) = (x + 3)(x - 7)$

C) $f(x) = (x - 2)^2 - 25$

D) $f(x) = x(x - 4) - 21$

10

$$p(x) = 3x^3 + 15x^2 + 18x$$
$$q(x) = x^2 + 5x + 6$$

The polynomials $p(x)$ and $q(x)$ are defined above. Which of the following polynomials is divisible by $3x - 2$?

A) $f(x) = p(x) - 2q(x)$

B) $g(x) = 2p(x) - 3q(x)$

C) $h(x) = 3p(x) - 2q(x)$

D) $j(x) = 4p(x) - 3q(x)$

9

ANSWERS AND EXPLANATIONS: PROBLEM SET 14

Easy

1. **B**   The question asks for which choice could be the graph of f if f has three distinct zeros. A zero is a point in which $y = 0$, or an x-intercept. Count the number of times the graph touches the x-axis in each choice. In (A), the graph touches the x-axis four times. In (B), the graph touches the x-axis three times. In (C), the graph touches the x-axis two times. In (D), the graph touches the x-axis two times. The answer is (B).

2. **A**   The question states that the function g has zeros at -4, 2, and 4. A zero is a point in which the value of the function is 0. Notice that each of the choices is in factored form. If k is a zero of a function, then $(x - k)$ is a factor of the function. Since the zeros of g are -4, 2, and 4, the factors of g must be $(x + 4)$, $(x - 2)$, and $(x - 4)$. Only (A) has all three factors. Alternatively, since -4, 2, and 4, are zeros, then $g(-4) = 0$, $g(2) = 0$, and $g(4) = 0$. Plug these points into each of the answer choices, crossing off any for which g is not 0. First, $g(4) = 0$ in (A), (B), and (C) but not (D), so eliminate (D). Then, $g(2) = 0$ in (A) and (B) but not (C), so eliminate (C). Finally, $g(-4) = 0$ in (A) but not (B), so eliminate (B). The answer is (A).

3. **B**   The question asks for the value of a. Since a is inside the parentheses, it is an x-value. When a function question asks for an x-value, Plug In the Answers. Start with (C). If $a = 2$, then $f(a) = f(2) = 2(2) + 1 = 5$. Since $f(a)$ should be 2, this is incorrect, so eliminate (C). Since the correct answer must be smaller, eliminate (D), as well. Now try (B). If $a = \frac{1}{2}$, then $f(a) = f\left(\frac{1}{2}\right) = 2\left(\frac{1}{2}\right) + 1 = 2$. Since this is what the question says $f(a)$ is, the answer is (B).

Medium

4. **C**   Don't do a lot of formula work. Think about how graphs work. In the equation, 2 represents the y-intercept, so eliminate any graphs that do not cross the y-axis at 2. You are down to (A) and (C). A slope of greater than 1 is relatively steep as compared with a 45-degree angle, while a fractional slope is relatively shallow. The slope here is 4, so you need a steep graph. Eliminate (A), and the answer is (C).

5. **D**   Don't do a lot of formula work. Think about how graphs work. The y-intercept on the graph is 3, so you need a formula that ends in $+3$. Eliminate (A) and (C). A slope of greater than 1 is relatively steep as compared with a 45-degree angle, while a fractional slope is relatively shallow. The slope of the lines on the graph is relatively steep, so eliminate (B), and the answer is (D).

6. **D** To determine a possible equation of the graph function, identify the zeroes, or the x-intercepts. The x-intercepts occur at $x = -4$, $x = 0$, and $x = 3$. If b is an x-intercept, then $(x - b)$ is a factor. Therefore, the factors of the equation of this function must be $(x + 4)$, (x), and $(x - 3)$. Eliminate the choices that do not have these three factors: (A) and (C). Look at the difference between (B) and (D). Both have factors of $(x + 4)$ and $(x - 3)$, but (B) has x, while (D) has x^2. There are two possible ways to determine which one it should be. One is to notice that at $x = 0$, the graph doesn't cross the x-axis but is tangent to it. This indicates a double root, or a root that is squared. Therefore, the equation must have x^2. The other way is to notice that the graph has three turning points. A graph must be of a degree that is at least one higher than the number of turning points. Therefore, this equation must be at least fourth degree. When an equation is in factored form, determine the degree by adding the degree of each factor. Choice (B) has three first degree factors, so it has a degree of $1 + 1 + 1 = 3$. Choice (D) has a second degree factor and two first degree factors, so it has a degree of $2 + 1 + 1 = 4$. Either way, the answer is (D).

7. **C** The question asks for where $f(x) = 0$, or where $2x^2 + 8x + 2 = 0$. To solve a quadratic in the form $ax^2 + bx + c = 0$, either factor or use the quadratic formula: $x = \dfrac{-b \pm \sqrt{b^2 - 4ac}}{2a}$. For a hint as to which to use, look at the answer choices. Since the answers more closely resemble the quadratic formula, use the quadratic formula. In this case, $a = 2$, $b = 8$, and $c = 2$. Plug these values into the quadratic formula to get $x = \dfrac{-8 \pm \sqrt{8^2 - 4(2)(2)}}{2(2)}$. Simplify to get $x = \dfrac{-8 \pm \sqrt{64 - 16}}{4}$ and $x = \dfrac{-8 \pm \sqrt{48}}{4}$. None of the choices include $\sqrt{48}$, so simplify the square root by finding a perfect square factor. List out the factors of 48: 1 and 48, 2 and 24, 3 and 16, 4 and 12, and 6 and 8. Of those factors, the greatest perfect square is 16. Therefore, $\sqrt{48} = \sqrt{16 \times 3} = \sqrt{16} \times \sqrt{3} = 4\sqrt{3}$. Substitute this to get $x = \dfrac{-8 \pm 4\sqrt{3}}{4}$. None of the answers have a

denominator of 4, so find a way to cancel the 4. To do so, factor a 4 from both terms in the numerator to get $x = \dfrac{4(-2 \pm \sqrt{3})}{4}$. Cancel the 4's to get $x = -2 \pm \sqrt{3}$. The answer is (C).

Hard

8. **D**   The easiest way to handle this is to understand how functions move. The −3 outside the parentheses shifts the original graph down by 3 units. Eliminate (C) because it is not shifted down. The +2 inside the parentheses shifts the original graph to the left by 2 units. Eliminate (A) and (B) because they are not shifted to the left. You can also Plug In, testing one of the points indicated by a dot against the function you are looking for.

9. **C**   The question asks for an equivalent form of the equation of the function in which the coordinates of the vertex can be found as constants. Therefore, the question is asking for the vertex form of the equation: $f(x) = a(x - h)^2 + k$, where (h, k) represents the vertex of the parabola. Eliminate any choice that is not in this form. Choices (A), (B), and (D) are not in vertex form, so eliminate them. Only one choice remains. Alternatively, find the vertex in the graph. The vertex is the minimum (or maximum) point on the graph and the point at which at parabola turns on the axis of symmetry. On the graph, this point appears to be at (2, −25). Eliminate any choices that do not have 2 and 25 as constants. Once again, this eliminates (A), (B), and (D). The answer is (C).

10. **A**   You could do a lot of algebraic manipulation and factoring to solve this, but there are variables everywhere, so Plug In. Pick a value for x such as $x = 3$. Find the values of p and q when $x = 3$. $p(3) = 3(3)^3 + 15(3)^2 + 18(3) = 81 + 135 + 54 = 270$. $q(3) = (3)^2 + 5(3) + 6 = 9 + 15 + 6 = 30$. The question asks for which of the given functions is divisible by $3x - 2$, so see which answer choices are divisible by $3(3) - 2 = 7$. In (A), $f(x) = p(x) - 2q(x)$, so when $x = 3$, $f(3) = 270 - 2(30) = 210$. This is divisible by 7, so keep (A). In (B), $g(3) = 2p(x) - 3q(x) = 2(270) - 3(30) = 450$. This is not divisible by 7, so eliminate it. In (C), $h(x) = 3p(x) - 2q(x) = 3(270) - 2(30) = 750$, and in (D), $j(x) = 4p(x) - 3q(x) = 4(270) - 3(30) = 990$. Neither of these are divisible by 7, so the answer is (A).

PROBLEM SET 15: GRID-INS

Easy

1

If $x - y = -6$, then y is how much greater than x?

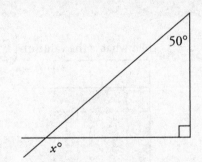

2

In the figure above, what is the value of x?

A certain solution requires $3\frac{1}{2}$ grams of additive for each 7 liters of water. At this rate, how many grams of additive should be used with 11 liters of water?

Medium

If $\left(\dfrac{x+2}{y+2}\right) = \dfrac{3}{4}$, then what is the value of $\left(\dfrac{2+y}{2+x}\right)^2$?

5

The speed, in miles per hour, of a particular experimental spacecraft t minutes after it is launched is modeled by the function M, which is defined as $M(t) = 200(3)^{\frac{t}{3}}$. According to this model, what is the speed, in miles per hour, 9 minutes after the spacecraft is launched?

6

Climate Preferences

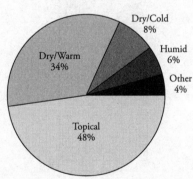

The graph above shows the results of a survey in which adults were asked to name their first preference among various types of climates. Of the adults surveyed, a total of 280 answered "Humid" or "Other." How many answered "Other" in the survey?

Hard

$$-4, 0, 2, 3$$

A sequence of numbers is formed by repeating the set of numbers until 80 numbers have been listed. What is the sum of the first 31 terms of the sequence?

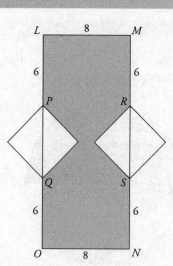

8

In the figure below, rectangle *LMNO* has dimensions of 18 by 8. Segments *PQ* and *RS* are diagonals of the squares shown. What is the area of the shaded region?

Questions 9 and 10 refer to the information below.

A scientist studies Bacteria Culture A, which grows ten percent every hour. Bacteria Culture A initially contained 200 microbes, and she models the growth using the equation $n = 200(m)^h$, where n is the number of microbes and h is the number of hours.

9

What is the value of m in the equation?

10

The same scientist also studies another culture, Bacteria Culture B, which grows 15% every hour. The two cultures began at the same time with the same number of microbes. After 20 hours, how many more microbes will Bacteria Culture B contain than Bacteria Culture A? (Round your answer to the nearest whole number.)

ANSWERS AND EXPLANATIONS: PROBLEM SET 15

Easy

1. **6**   Set the equation equal to y, since that's what the question asks for. You get $-y = -6 - x$. Multiply through by -1 and you get $y = 6 + x$, so the answer is 6. For an easier solution, you could also Plug In here: Say $x = 2$ and $y = 8$, which satisfies the equation. Then y is equal to x plus 6.

2. **140**   The unmarked angle in the triangle is 40°, since triangles have 180° and the other angles are 50° and 90°. The 40° angle and x lie on a straight line, so $40 + x = 180$, and $x = 140$.

3. **5.5**   You can set up the proportions as follows and cross-multiply:

$$\frac{3.5 \text{ g}}{7 \text{ l}} = \frac{x}{11 \text{ l}}$$

Cross-multiply to get $7x = 38.5$. Divide both sides by 7 to get $x = 5.5$. However, if you noticed that the number of grams is one-half the number of liters (not accounting for units), then all you need to do is divide 11 by 2.

Medium

4. $\dfrac{16}{9}$ This is a good example of plugging in on a grid-in question. If you make $x = 1$ and $y = 2$, the equation will work:

$$\left(\frac{1 + 2}{2 + 2}\right) = \frac{3}{4}$$

Now it is easy to solve the problem. By the way, if you noticed that $\left(\dfrac{2 + y}{2 + x}\right)$ is the reciprocal of $\left(\dfrac{x + 2}{y + 2}\right)$, you didn't need to Plug In. Just square $\dfrac{4}{3}$!

5. **5400** This question asks you to plug $t = 9$ into the given formula:

$$M(t) = 200(3)^{\frac{9}{3}} = 200(3)^3 = 200(27) = 5,400.$$

6. **112** Make sure you understand the information you are given and the information you need to find before trying to answer the question. There are 280 people who answered "Humid" or "Other," not 280 total people, so don't take 10 percent of 280. Also, there is no need to calculate the total number of people surveyed. Of the people who answered "Humid" and "Other," 4 out of 10 answered "Other." Thus, the number of people who answer "Other" is $\frac{4}{10}$ of 280, or 112.

Hard

7. **5** If you are stumped here, you can always type the pattern into your calculator and find the answer. However, on pattern questions, once you understand how the pattern operates, you can arrive at the answer faster. Here, add up the first four numbers of the repeating sequence. They add up to 1. Thus, every time you add another set of the sequence, the total sum will increase by 1. Because you are interested in the first 31 terms of the sequence, there will be 7 complete sets (the first 28 terms) added together and then part of a set (the remaining 3 terms). Those 7 complete sets will add up to 7. So now add in -4, 0, and 2 to get $7 - 4 + 0 + 2 = 5$.

8. **126** Without answer choices, you can't Ballpark, so you need to slog through! The area of the entire rectangle is 144 (18 × 8). Now you need to find the area of the triangles inside of the rectangle. You can see that the measurements on either side of the squares are all 6 and the entire length of the rectangle is 18, so the portion of the rectangle inside each square is also 6. When a square is cut in half along its diagonal, two 45-45-90 triangles are created. If you don't know how 45-45-90 triangles work, you can look up the ratio in the formula box at the beginning of the section. If each side of the triangle (here, the sides of the square) is x, the hypotenuse (here, the diagonal) is $x\sqrt{2}$. Thus, here $6 = x\sqrt{2}$, so $x = \dfrac{6}{\sqrt{2}}$. Now that you have the sides of the squares, you can find the areas of the squares: $\dfrac{6}{\sqrt{2}} \times \dfrac{6}{\sqrt{2}} = \dfrac{36}{2} = 18$. Because the two triangles inside the rectangle add up to one square, you can subtract 18 from 144 to find the area of the shaded region.

9. **1.1** The equation $n = 200(m)^h$ is in the form of the standard equation for exponential growth: *final amount = original amount*$(1 + rate)^{number\ of\ changes}$, where *rate* is the percent in decimal form. The *final amount* is n, the *original amount* is 200, and the *number of changes* is h. Therefore, m from the original equation represents $1 + rate$ from the standard equation. Since the increase per hour is 10%, $m = 1 + 0.10 = 1.1$. The answer is 1.1.

10. **1928** The question asks for how many more microbes Bacteria Culture B contains than Bacteria Culture A after 20 hours. As we just saw in the previous question, m, the rate of increase, is equal to 1.1 for Bacteria Culture A and 1.15 for Bacteria Culture B. After $h = 20$ hours, Bacteria Culture A has $n = 200(1.1)^{20} \approx 1{,}345.5$ microbes, and Bacteria Culture B has $n = 200(1.15)^{20} \approx 3{,}273.3$ microbes. Therefore, after 20 hours, Bacteria Culture B has $3{,}273.3 - 1{,}345.5 = 1{,}927.8$ more microbes than Bacteria Culture A. The question asks for this to be rounded to the nearest whole number, so the answer is 1,928.

PROBLEM SET 16: MORE GRID-INS

Easy

1

If $2x - 3y = 7$ and $y = 3$, then what is the value of x ?

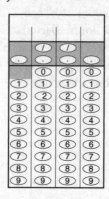

2

In the figure above, if $a = 170$, what is the value of b ?

At a certain beach, the cost of renting a beach umbrella is $4.25 per day or $28.00 per week. If Kelly and Brandon rent a beach umbrella for 2 weeks instead of renting one each day for 14 days, how much money, in dollars, will they save? (Leave off the dollar sign when gridding in your answer.)

Medium

The average (arithmetic mean) of 8 numbers is 65. If one of the numbers, 65, is removed, what is the average of the remaining 7 numbers?

5

The face of a wall measures 30 yards by 24 yards. If the wall is to be completely covered with square bricks measuring 3 yards on each side, how many bricks will be needed to cover the wall?

6

In a recent marathon, 70 percent of those who entered the race reached the finish line. If 720 did not reach the finish line, how many people entered the race?

Hard

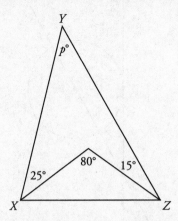

Note: Figure not drawn to scale.

In triangle *XYZ* above, what is the value of *p* ?

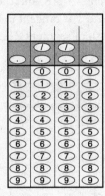

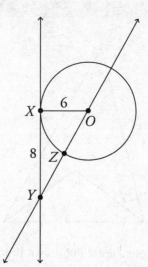

In the figure above, O is the center of the circle, the length of segment XY is 8, and the line passing through points X and Y is tangent to the circle at point X. What is the length of segment ZY ?

Let the function g be defined as $g(x) = -3x + 6$. If $g(6) = r$, what is the value of $g(r)$?

When a number is subtracted from 8 less than three times the number, the result is 142. What is the number?

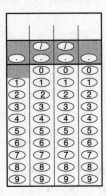

ANSWERS AND EXPLANATIONS: PROBLEM SET 16

Easy

1. **8** The problem tells you that $y = 3$, so plug that into the equation and you get $2x - 9 = 7$. So $2x = 16$ and $x = 8$.

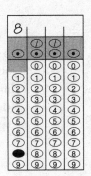

2. **10** Write 170° next to a. There are 180° in a line, so $b = 10$.

3. **3.50** Kelly and Brandon spent $28 per week for 2 weeks for a total of $56. If they had rented the umbrella by the day, they would've spent 14 × $4.25 for a total of $59.50. That means they saved 59.50 − 56 = 3.50.

Medium

4. **65** You can use the Average Pie: 8 (the number of items) times 65 (the average) gives you a sum of 520. If you subtract 65, the new sum is 455. Divide 455 by 7 (the new number of items) to get the new average: 65. You can also think about this logically: If all 8 numbers were 65, and one of those numbers were removed, the remaining 7 numbers would still average 65.

5. **80** To find out how many bricks will fit on the wall, you need to divide the dimensions of the wall by the dimensions of the bricks:

$$\frac{30 \times 24}{3 \times 3} = \frac{720}{9} = 80$$

6. **2400** Translate the question to create an equation that you can solve. If 70% of the runners finished, then 30% did not. So the question is asking, "720 is 30% of what number?" As an equation, that translates to $720 = 0.3x$. Divide both sides by 0.3 to find that $x = 2,400$.

Hard

7. **40** This figure is not drawn to scale, so be careful as you fill in the information you need. In order to find the value of *p*, you need to find the sum of angles *YXZ* and *YZX*. You are given some information about those angles: the measurements 25 and 15 above the smaller triangle. However, because the figure is not drawn to scale, there is no way to determine the missing measurements. That said, it doesn't matter what angles *YXZ* and *YZX* actually are. Only their sum is important. So, let's look at the smaller triangle. The top vertex is 80, which means that the sum of the bottom vertices is 100. Plug in some numbers, such as 50 and 50. Now you have measures for *YXZ* and *YZX*: 75 and 65, for a sum of 140. Subtract that from 180 to find angle *p* : 180 − 140 = 40.

8. **4** To get this question right, you need to know that a line tangent to a circle forms a right angle with the radius at the point of tangency. Thus, triangle *XOY* is a right triangle. You can use the Pythagorean Theorem or recognize the 6-8-10 triangle to find that the hypotenuse is 10. You're not done yet, though. To find *YZ*, you need to subtract the length of *OZ* from 10. *OZ* is a radius, just as is *OX*. As *OX* is 6, so is *OZ*, leaving 4 for *ZY*.

9. **42** When you are given a function, always take the number inside the parentheses and plug it into the function. Here, you must plug 6 into the function:

$$g(6) = -3(6) + 6 = -18 + 6 = -12$$

Thus, *r* = −12. Are you worried that there is no way to grid in a negative number? Actually, you are not done. The question asks for *g(r)*, not *g(6)*. Knowing that *r* = −12, you can plug that number into the function:

$$g(-12) = -3(-12) + 6 = 36 + 6 = 42$$

10.   **125**   You need to translate English into Math. Let's call "a number" x. You need to subtract x from 8 less than 3 times x. Three times x is $3x$. To find the number 8 less than $3x$, you need to subtract 8. Thus, putting it all together, you get:

$$(3x - 8) - x$$

You are told that the result of this operation is 142, so:

$$(3x - 8) - x = 142$$

Now, you can solve for x:

$$2x - 8 = 142$$
$$2x = 150$$
$$x = 125$$

PROBLEM SET 17: MIXED BAG

Easy

1

If $x = 14 - y$, what is $3x$ when $y = 11$?

A) −9

B) −3

C) 3

D) 9

2

At Rose's Flower Shop, the cost of purchasing a bundle of 8 ferns is $57. The cost of each fern, when purchased separately, is $9. How much money would be saved by purchasing a bundle of 8 ferns, rather than purchasing 8 ferns separately?

A) 12

B) 13

C) 14

D) 15

3

In isosceles triangle *ABC*, one angle measures 55° and another angle measures 70°. Which one of the following is the measure of the third angle?

A) 40

B) 55

C) 70

D) It cannot be determined from the information given.

Medium

4

If $24b^2 - 4x = 32$, what is the value of $6b^2 - x$?

A) 6

B) 8

C) 12

D) 16

5

Sasha has a collection of 60 vinyl records, some of which are classic jazz and the rest of which are hip hop. If Sasha has $\frac{1}{4}$ as many classic jazz records as she has hip hop records, how many classic jazz records does she have?

A) 12

B) 15

C) 45

D) 48

6

If p is an integer such that $-5 < p < 5$ and $q = 3p - p^3$, what is the least possible value of q ?

A) −76

B) −52

C) −4

D) 0

Hard

7

In terms of x, what is the difference between $6x + 9$ and $2x - 4$, if $x > 2$?

A) $3x + 5$

B) $4x - 5$

C) $4x + 5$

D) $4x + 13$

8

In triangle ABC, the measures of angles a, b, and c, respectively, are in the ratio 2:3:4. What is the measure of angle b ?

A) 20

B) 40

C) 60

D) 80

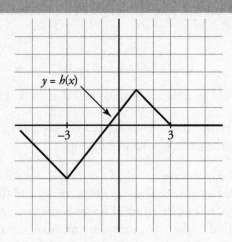

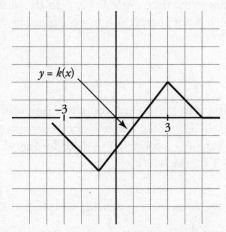

The graphs above show the complete functions h and k. Which one of the following expresses $k(x)$ in terms of $h(x)$?

A) $k(x) = h(x) + 2$

B) $k(x) = h(x) - 2$

C) $k(x) = h(x + 2)$

D) $k(x) = h(x - 2)$

If $h^{\frac{2}{3}} = k^2$, then in terms of k, what is the value of h^2 ?

A) $k^{\frac{2}{3}}$

B) $k^{\frac{4}{9}}$

C) k^3

D) k^6

ANSWERS AND EXPLANATIONS: PROBLEM SET 17

Easy

1. **D**   Plug $y = 11$ into the equation to find that $x = 3$. Therefore, $3x = 9$.

2. **D**   Calculate the cost of buying 8 ferns separately: $8 \times 9 = 72$. Now, subtract the package price of 57 from 72.

3. **B**   In an isosceles triangle, two of three angles are the same. Thus, the only two possible numerical answers here are (B) and (C). Before you decide that it cannot be determined between the two answers, try them out. If the third angle is 55, then the sum of all three angles is 180. That works. But if the third angle is 70, then the sum of all three angles is 195, which is not possible in a triangle. The answer is therefore (B).

Medium

4. **B**   Before you start performing complex manipulations and calculations, ask yourself "Of all the questions in the world, why ask for $6b^2 - x$?" The answer: $6b^2 - x$ is just $24b^2 - 4x$ divided by 4! Therefore, the answer is $32 \div 4 = 8$, which is (B).

5. **A**   Plug In the Answers here, starting with (C). If she has 45 classic jazz albums and this represents $\frac{1}{4}$ of the number of hip hop albums she has, she would have 180 hip hop albums. This is way too big. The answer must be smaller, so eliminate (C) and (D). Try (B). If she has 15 classic jazz albums, she has 60 hip hop albums. 60 should be the total, not just the number of hip hop albums, so eliminate (B). For (A), she would have 48 hip hop albums—for a total of 60.

6. **B**   There are only 9 possible values of p between -5 and 5. Since there are relatively few values, it may be easiest to plug in all possible values of p. If $p = -4$, then $3p - p^3 = 52$. If $p = -3$, then $3p - p^3 = 18$. If $p = -2$, then $3p - p^3 = 2$. If $p = -1$, then $3p - p^3 = -2$. If $p = 0$, then $3p - p^3 = 0$. If $p = 1$, then $3p - p^3 = 2$. If $p = 2$, then $3p - p^3 = -2$. If $p = 3$, then $3p - p^3 = -18$. If $p = 4$, then $3p - p^3 = -52$. The least possible value is -52, so the answer is (B).

Hard

7. **D** Plug In. If $x = 3$, then $6x + 9 = 27$ and $2x - 4 = 2$. The difference is 25. Plug 3 into the answer choices, eliminating any choice that doesn't give you 25. Choice (A) is $3(3) + 5 = 14$, so eliminate (A). Choice (B) is $4(3) - 5 = 7$, so eliminate (B). Choice (C) is $4(3) + 5 = 17$, so eliminate (C). Choice (D) is $4(3) + 13 = 25$. Since (D) is the only choice that resulted in 25, it is the answer.

8. **C** Create a Ratio Box. For the actual total, use 180, as there are 180° in a triangle. Your completed Ratio Box will look like this:

	a	b	c	Total
Ratio	2	3	4	9
Multiplier	20	20	20	20
Actual Numbers	40	60	80	180

The question asks for the measure of angle b, which is 60, so the answer is (C).

9. **D** The easiest way to answer this question is to understand transformation of graphs. Just count how many units the graph moved. It moved 2 units to the right but did not move up or down. When a graph moves to the right, you need to subtract the number of units from x *inside* the parentheses.

10. **D** If you are comfortable manipulating equations with exponents, first isolate h by raising $h^{\frac{2}{3}}$ to the power of $\frac{3}{2}$. Having done so on the left side of the equation, you must do the same on the right side. Thus, you get: $h = k^3$. The question, however, asks for h^2, not x, so square both sides, using the Power-Multiply Rule to get $h^2 = (k^3)^2 = k^6$. As an alternative, understand that $h^{\frac{2}{3}} = \sqrt[3]{h^2}$, so you can cube both sides to get $h^2 = (k^2)^3$, which leads you down the same steps of then using the Power-Multiply Rule to get $h^2 = k^6$.

PROBLEM SET 18: MORE MIXED BAG

Easy

1

For $i = \sqrt{-1}$, what is the sum of $(5 + 2i) + (-7 + 3i)$?

A) $-2 - i$

B) $-2 + 5i$

C) $12 - i$

D) $12 + 5i$

2

If n and s are integers, and $n + 5 < 7$, and $s - 6 < -4$, which of the following could be a value of $n + s$?

A) 2

B) 3

C) 4

D) 6

3

A home designer will carpet n rooms with the same dimensions in a house using a specific type of carpeting. The designer charges using the expression $nClw$, where n is the number of rooms, C is a constant with units of dollars per square meter, l is the length of each room in meters, and w is the width of each room in meters. If a customer asks the designer to use a less expensive type of carpeting, which of the following factors in the expression would change?

A) n

B) C

C) l

D) w

Medium

Which of the following lines is perpendicular to
$y = 2x + 7$?

A) $y = 3x + \dfrac{1}{7}$

B) $y = 3x - \dfrac{1}{7}$

C) $y = -\dfrac{1}{2}x + 3$

D) $y = \dfrac{1}{2}x + 3$

Which of the following complex numbers is
equivalent to $\dfrac{7 - 3i}{2 + 4i}$?

(Note: $i = \sqrt{-1}$)

A) $\dfrac{1}{10} - \dfrac{17i}{10}$

B) $\dfrac{1}{10} + \dfrac{17i}{10}$

C) $\dfrac{7}{2} - \dfrac{3i}{4}$

D) $\dfrac{7}{2} + \dfrac{3i}{4}$

The total cost, y, for Rosa to go on vacation for x days
is given by the equation $y = A + (H + M)x$, where A
represents the airfare, H represents the cost per day
for the hotel, and M represents the cost of meals. If the
relationship between the total cost of the vacation and
the number of days of the vacation is graphed on the
xy-plane, what does the slope of the line represent?

A) The total cost daily cost of the hotel and meals

B) The total daily cost of the vacation

C) The total cost of the hotel and meals

D) The total cost of the vacation

7

A bank account pays interest at an annual rate of 4%. If the initial deposit on the account is $1,250 and no other deposits or withdrawal are made to the account, which of the following functions A models the amount of money in the bank account after y years?

A) $A(y) = 0.04(1,250)^y$

B) $A(y) = 1.04(1,250)^y$

C) $A(y) = 1,250(0.04)^y$

D) $A(y) = 1,250(1.04)^y$

HARD

8

$$x^2 + y^2 - 6x + 8y = -9$$

The equation of a circle in the xy-plane is shown above. What is the radius of the circle?

A) 3

B) 4

C) 9

D) 16

Questions 9 and 10 refer to the following information.

In a certain company, 55% of the employees are male. 64% of the female employees and 58% of the male employees receive year-end raises.

9

What percent of the employees at the company receive year-end raises?

(Ignore the percent symbol when entering your answer. For example, if the answer is 42.1%, enter 42.1.)

What percent of the employees who receive raises are female? (Ignore the percent symbol when entering your answer. For example, if the answer is 42.1%, enter 42.1.)

ANSWERS AND EXPLANATIONS: PROBLEM SET 18

Easy

1. **B**   To add complex numbers, just treat i like a variable and combine like terms: $5 + (-7) = 5 - 7 = -2$ and $2i + 3i = 5i$. Therefore, $(5 + 2i) + (-7 + 3i) = -2 + 5i$. The answer is (B).

2. **A**   First, fix the ranges. You can see $n < 2$ and $s < 2$. Since they both must be integers, the greatest either n or s could be is 1. $1 + 1$ is 2, so that is the only answer that works.

3. **B**   To determine which factor would change with a less expensive type of carpeting, determine the meaning of each variable in the expression. Choice (A) is n, which represents the number of rooms. This does not change when the type of carpeting changes, so eliminate (A). Choice (B) is C, which is a constant, with units of dollars per square meter. Since this seems to be related to the cost of the carpet, keep (B). Choice (C) is l, which represents the length of each room. The length would not change with a different type of carpet, so eliminate (C). Choice (D) is w, which represents the width of each room. The width would not change with a different type of carpet, so eliminate (D). Only one choice remains. The answer is (B).

Medium

4. **C**   In the form $y = mx + b$, m is the slope, which means that the line given by the equation $y = 2x + 7$ has a slope of 2. A line perpendicular to $y = 2x + 7$ will have a slope that is the negative reciprocal to 2. Choice (C) has a slope of $-\frac{1}{2}$.

5.   **A**   To simplify a fraction of complex numbers, multiply the numerator and denominator by the conjugate of the denominator. The conjugate is the same expression, but with the opposite sign between terms. In this case, the denominator is $2 + 4i$, so the conjugate of the denominator is $2 - 4i$. Multiply the numerator and denominator by this conjugate to get $\frac{7 - 3i}{2 + 4i} \times \frac{2 - 4i}{2 - 4i}$. FOIL both the numerator and denominator to get $\frac{14 - 28i - 6i + 12i^2}{4 - 8i + 8i - 16i^2}$. Combine like terms to get $\frac{14 - 34i + 12i^2}{4 - 16i^2}$. By definition, $i^2 = -1$, so substitute this to get $\frac{14 - 34i + 12(-1)}{4 - 16(-1)} = \frac{14 - 34i - 12}{4 + 16}$. Combine like terms again to get $\frac{2 - 34i}{20}$. Since each of the answer choices is in the form of two fractions, break up the fraction to get $\frac{2}{20} - \frac{34i}{20}$. Reduce both fractions by 2 to get $\frac{1}{10} - \frac{17i}{10}$. The answer is (A).

6.   **A**   Rewrite the equation $y = A + (H + M)x$ in $y = mx + b$ form, where m represents the slope of the line and b represents the y-intercept. To do this, simply reverse the order of the terms to get $y = (H + M)x + A$. When the question asks what the slope represents, it's really asking for the meaning of $(H + M)$. Since H represents the daily cost of the hotel and M represents the daily cost of meals, $H + M$ represents the total daily cost of these two things together. The answer is (A).

7.   **D**   Interest is an example of exponential growth, which uses the formula *final amount* = *original amount*$(1 + rate)^{number\ of\ changes}$. The *original amount* is the initial deposit, which is 1,250. The *rate* is 4% written in decimal form, which is 0.04. Because the account pays annual interest, the *number of changes* is the number of years, which is y. Therefore, the amount of money in the account after y years is $1{,}250(1 + 0.04)^y = 1{,}250(1.04)^y$. The answer is (D).

Hard

8. **B** To find the radius of the circle from the equation, get the equation in the standard form for a circle: $(x - h)^2 + (y - k)^2 = r^2$, where (h, k) represents the center of the circle and r represents the radius. To do this, complete the square. Start by grouping the terms with x and grouping the terms with y to get $(x^2 - 6x) + (y^2 + 8y) = -9$. Now take half of the coefficient on x and square it. In this case, the coefficient on x is -6. Half of the coefficient is -3, and the square is 9. Add 9 to both sides to get $(x^2 - 6x + 9) + (y^2 + 8y) = -9 + 9$. Do the same for the coefficient on y. The coefficient on y is 8. Half of 8 is 4, and the square of 4 is 16. Add 16 to both sides to get $(x^2 - 6x + 9) + (y^2 + 8y + 16) = -9 + 9 + 16$. Simplify the right side to get $(x^2 - 6x + 9) + (y^2 + 8y + 16) = 16$. Factor the x terms to get $(x - 3)^2 + (y^2 + 8y + 16) = 16$. Factor the y terms to get $(x - 3)^2 + (y + 4)^2 = 16$. Note that completing the square is a deliberate effort to get a quadratic that is the square of a binomial, so there will always be a way to get the equation in this form. The question asks for the radius. The question is in the form $(x - h)^2 + (y - k)^2 = r^2$, so $r^2 = 16$. Take the square root of both sides to get $r = 4$. The answer is (B).

9. **60.7** The question asks for percents, so plug in 100 for the total number of employees. The question says that 55% of the employees are male, so there are 55 male employees and 45 female employees. If 64% of the female employees receive a raise, then $\frac{64}{100} \times 45 = 28.8$ female employees receive a raise. This is a decimal but that's fine. While you can't have fractions of people in the real world, the math will work out fine for this problem and you won't have to stress about finding a perfect number to plug in. If 58% of male employees receive a raise, then $\frac{58}{100} \times 55 = 31.9$ male employees receive a raise. Therefore, a total of $28.8 + 31.9 = 60.7$ employees receive a raise. Since the total number of employees is 100, 60.7 employees represents 60.7%. The answer is 60.7.

10.　**47.4** The question asks what percent of the employees who receive raises are female, so determine $\frac{\text{female raises}}{\text{total raises}} \times 100$. If you did the work for the previous question, you already have some numbers to work with. According to our previous calculations, there are 28.8 females who get raises out of 60.7 total employees who get raises. Therefore, $\frac{\text{female raises}}{\text{total raises}} \times 100 = \frac{28.8}{60.7} \times 100 = 47.446$. Unless otherwise specified, always enter as many digits as you can into the grid-in box: The answer is 47.4.

NOTES

NOTES

NOTES

International Offices Listing

China (Beijing)
1501 Building A,
Disanji Creative Zone,
No.66 West Section of North 4th Ring Road Beijing
Tel: +86-10-62684481/2/3
Email: tprkor01@chol.com
Website: www.tprbeijing.com

China (Shanghai)
1010 Kaixuan Road
Building B, 5/F
Changning District, Shanghai, China 200052
Sara Beattie, Owner: Email: tprenquiry.sha@sarabeattie.com
Tel: +86-21-5108-2798
Fax: +86-21-6386-1039
Website: www.princetonreviewshanghai.com

Hong Kong
5th Floor, Yardley Commercial Building
1–6 Connaught Road West, Sheung Wan, Hong Kong
(MTR Exit C)
Sara Beattie, Owner: Email: tprenquiry.sha@sarabeattie.com
Tel: +852-2507-9380
Fax: +852-2827-4630
Website: www.princetonreviewhk.com

India (Mumbai)
Score Plus Academy
Office No.15, Fifth Floor
Manek Mahal 90
Veer Nariman Road
Next to Hotel Ambassador
Churchgate, Mumbai 400020
Maharashtra, India
Ritu Kalwani: Email: director@score-plus.com
Tel: + 91 22 22846801 / 39 / 41
Website: www.scoreplusindia.com

India (New Delhi)
South Extension
K–16, Upper Ground Floor
South Extension Part–1,
New Delhi-110049
Aradhana Mahna: aradhana@manyagroup.com
Monisha Banerjee: monisha@manyagroup.com
Ruchi Tomar: ruchi.tomar@manyagroup.com
Rishi Josan: Rishi.josan@manyagroup.com
Vishal Goswamy: vishal.goswamy@manyagroup.com
Tel: +91-11-64501603/ 4, +91-11-65028379
Website: www.manyagroup.com

Lebanon
463 Bliss Street
AlFarra Building–2nd floor
Ras Beirut
Beirut, Lebanon
Hassan Coudsi: Email: hassan.coudsi@review.com
Tel: +961-1-367-688
Website: www.princetonreviewlebanon.com

Korea
945-25 Young Shin Building
25 Daechi-Dong, Kangnam-gu
Seoul, Korea 135-280
Yong-Hoon Lee: Email: TPRKor01@chollian.net
In-Woo Kim: Email: iwkim@tpr.co.kr
Tel: + 82-2-554-7762
Fax: +82-2-453-9466
Website: www.tpr.co.kr

Kuwait
ScorePlus Learning Center
Salmiyah Block 3, Street 2 Building 14
Post Box: 559, Zip 1306, Safat, Kuwait
Email: infokuwait@score-plus.com
Tel: +965-25-75-48-02 / 8
Fax: +965-25-75-46-02
Website: www.scorepluseducation.com

Malaysia
Sara Beattie MDC Sdn Bhd
Suites 18E & 18F
18th Floor
Gurney Tower, Persiaran Gurney
Penang, Malaysia
Email: tprkl.my@sarabeattie.com
Sara Beattie, Owner: Email: tprenquiry.sha@sarabeattie.com
Tel: +604-2104 333
Fax: +604-2104 330
Website: www.princetonreviewKL.com

Mexico
TPR México
Guanajuato No. 242 Piso 1 Interior 1
Col. Roma Norte
México D.F., C.P.06700
registro@princetonreviewmexico.com
Tel: +52-55-5255-4495
+52-55-5255-4440
+52-55-5255-4442
Website: www.princetonreviewmexico.com

Qatar
Score Plus
Villa No. 49, Al Waab Street
Opp Al Waab Petrol Station
Post Box: 39068, Doha, Qatar
Email: infoqatar@score-plus.com
Tel: +974 44 36 8580, +974 526 5032
Fax: +974 44 13 1995
Website: www.scorepluseducation.com

Taiwan
The Princeton Review Taiwan
2F, 169 Zhong Xiao East Road, Section 4
Taipei, Taiwan 10690
Lisa Bartle (Owner): lbartle@princetonreview.com.tw
Tel: +886-2-2751-1293
Fax: +886-2-2776-3201
Website: www.PrincetonReview.com.tw

Thailand
The Princeton Review Thailand
Sathorn Nakorn Tower, 28th floor
100 North Sathorn Road
Bangkok, Thailand 10500
Thavida Bijayendrayodhin (Chairman)
Email: thavida@princetonreviewthailand.com
Mitsara Bijayendrayodhin (Managing Director)
Email: mitsara@princetonreviewthailand.com
Tel: +662-636-6770
Fax: +662-636-6776
Website: www.princetonreviewthailand.com

Turkey
Yeni Sülün Sokak No. 28
Levent, Istanbul, 34330, Turkey
Nuri Ozgur: nuri@tprturkey.com
Rona Ozgur: rona@tprturkey.com
Iren Ozgur: iren@tprturkey.com
Tel: +90-212-324-4747
Fax: +90-212-324-3347
Website: www.tprturkey.com

UAE
Emirates Score Plus
Office No: 506, Fifth Floor
Sultan Business Center
Near Lamcy Plaza, 21 Oud Metha Road
Post Box: 44098, Dubai
United Arab Emirates
Hukumat Kalwani: skoreplus@gmail.com
Ritu Kalwani: director@score-plus.com
Email: info@score-plus.com
Tel: +971-4-334-0004
Fax: +971-4-334-0222
Website: www.scorepluseducation.com

Our International Partners

The Princeton Review also runs courses with a variety of partners in Africa, Asia, Europe, and South America.

Georgia
LEAF American-Georgian Education Center
www.leaf.ge

Mongolia
English Academy of Mongolia
www.nyescm.org

Nigeria
The Know Place
www.knowplace.com.ng

Panama
Academia Interamericana de Panama
http://aip.edu.pa/

Switzerland
Institut Le Rosey
http://www.rosey.ch/

All other inquiries, please email us at
internationalsupport@review.com